MEL BAY PRESENTS

Baroque Music for Acoustic Guitar

BY STEPHEN C. SIKTBERG

1 2 3 4 5 6 7 8 9 0

Visit us on the Web at www.melbay.com — E-mail us at email@melbay.com

Table of Contents

George Philip Telemann (1681-1776)

George Friedrich Handel (1685-1759)

Johann Sebastian Bach (1685-1750)

Foreword

The musical selections in this book come from some of the greatest composers of the Baroque Period. Since none of these individuals wrote for the guitar, these pieces are arrangements of works originally intended for other instruments.

In selecting material for this book, I was careful to choose pieces that could be played on the guitar without straying too much from the original versions. The most frequent alterations I made were either to change the key, change the register of the bass line, or occasionally revoice a chord.

A very important aspect of the performance of Baroque music is the use of ornamentation. Though often represented by symbols in the score, ornaments are sometimes implied by the musical context. The most common types are trills, though there are many others. Their execution is flexible and open to the interpretation of the performer.

For the purposes of this book (and after doing considerable research), I have written out all of the ornaments in conventional notation. As such, these realizations have been subject to my interpretation. In some cases, where a particular ornament is prohibitively difficult on the guitar, it has been either modified or omitted.

About the Composers

Johann Pachelbel (1653-1706) was a German organist and composer who is best known today for his "Canon in D." The fugues that are included here were written for the organ but work well on the guitar. The early Baroque style of writing in these pieces is less chromatic than in the fugues of Bach, and is reminiscent of the ricercares and fantasies for lute that were popular in the Renaissance.

The most famous composer of late 17th-century England was Henry Purcell (1659-1695). His influence can be heard in the music of Handel, who spent the better part of his professional life in England. Purcell is perhaps best known for his choral works though he wrote music of all types. The pieces here are taken from his miscellaneous keyboard compositions.

Francois Couperin (1668-1733) was an internationally famous French composer and harpsichord virtuoso. He was one of the first proponents of the rococo or "gallant" style which was simpler and more elegant than mainstream Baroque music and ultimately helped pave the way for the early Classical composers.

Like Couperin, Jean-Philippe Rameau (1683-1764) was a famous French composer who wrote in the "gallant" style. He is considered by many to be the father of the study of harmony because of his many writings on the subject. His three collections of harpsichord pieces are the source for the arrangements in this volume.

The keyboard sonatas of Domenico Scarlatti (1685-1757) have long been a favorite with guitarists. He wrote over five hundred of them, many of which fit well on the guitar. Though he was born in Italy, he spent his last years in Spain where the sonatas included here were written.

George Philip Telemann (1681-1776), was a very prolific and successful German composer who was friends with both Bach and Handel. The pieces here are taken from his 36 Fantasias for Harpsichord. The style of writing in these pieces varies from the Baroque to the Rococo.

Johann Sebastian Bach (1685-1750) and George Friedrich Handel (1685-1759) are often mentioned in the same breath as representing the pinnacle of Baroque music. Although Handel, like Bach, was born and raised in Germany, he spent most of his life in England where he became a citizen and wrote his most famous works. His keyboard pieces offer an interesting contrast to those of Bach and often fit nicely on the guitar.

Bach was most famous in his lifetime as an organist and wasn't appreciated as one of the greatest musical geniuses of all time until years later. His music is a staple of the classical guitar repertoire and many editions of his works are available. The selections included here are taken from his sonatas and partitas for solo violin and suites for violoncello. They will be familiar to classical guitarists, although the keys selected here are lower than is customary. Using the lower register of the instrument helps eliminate the need for extra bass notes, which results in arrangements that are easier to play and, in some cases, closer to Bach's original versions.

About the Notation

The arrangements in this book are for the guitarist with intermediate to advanced finger-style technique, and can be played on both nylon and steel-string instruments. Tablature has been included for those who prefer it over standard notation.

Barres are indicated by Roman numerals that represent the fret numbers and are accompanied by a fraction when only a partial barre is required. A solid line following the Roman numeral indicates the barre's duration while a dotted line accompanied by the abbreviation "h. b." represents a hinge (partially lifted) barre. Natural harmonics are indicated by a diamond over or under a note and the abbreviation "n. h." Circled numbers indicate which string a note or sequence of notes should be played on.

Left-hand fingering has been included extensively whereas right-hand fingering has been in most cases left up to the performer. Requirements for altered tunings and suggestions for the use of a capo are indicated at the beginning of each piece where applicable. The metronome settings are editorial and need not be followed exactly. Enjoy!

Fugue in C

Johann Pachelbel
(arranged for guitar
by Stephen C. Siktberg)

Fugue in G

Johann Pachelbel
(arranged for guitar
by Stephen C. Siktberg)

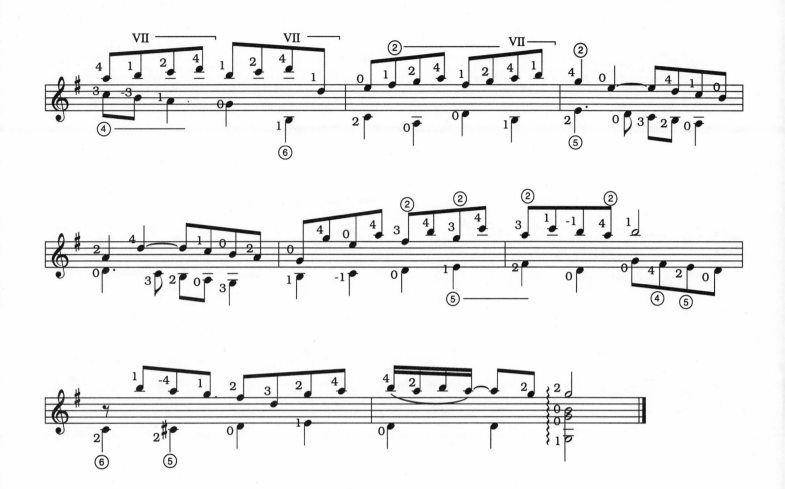

Fugue in G

Johann Pachelbel
(arranged for guitar
by Stephen C. Siktberg)

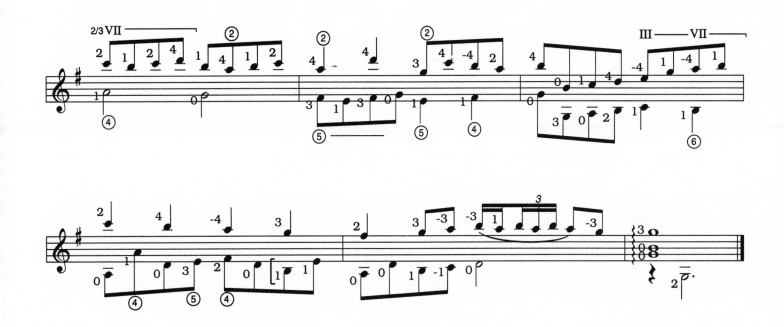

Fugue in Dm

6th = D

Johann Pachelbel
(arranged for guitar
by Stephen C. Siktberg)

14

Fugue in D

6th = D

Johann Pachelbel
(arranged for guitar
by Stephen C. Siktberg)

17

Air in Em

Henry Purcell
(arranged for guitar
by Stephen C. Siktberg)

(♩ = 130)

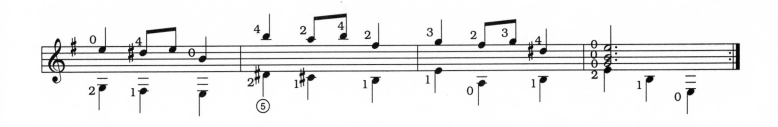

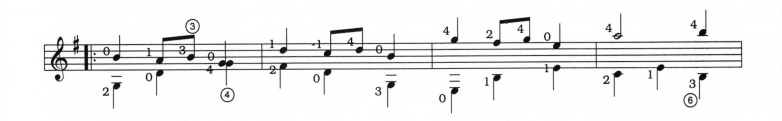

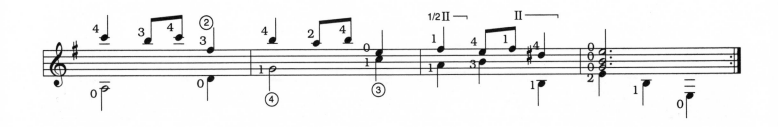

Hornpipe in Em

Henry Purcell
(arranged for guitar
by Stephen C. Siktberg)

Prelude

6th = D

Henry Purcell
(arranged for guitar
by Stephen C. Siktberg)

Prelude

Henry Purcell
(arranged for guitar
by Stephen C. Siktberg)

6th = D

March in D

Henry Purcell
(arranged for guitar
by Stephen C. Siktberg)

A Ground in G

Henry Purcell
(arranged for guitar
by Stephen C. Siktberg)

25

26

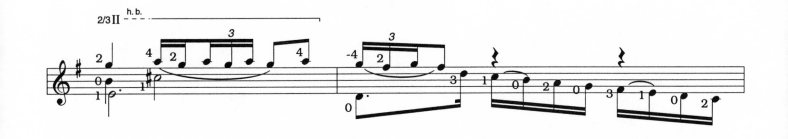

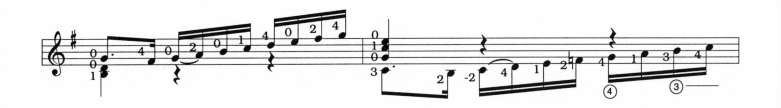

Air in Em

Henry Purcell
(arranged for guitar
by Stephen C. Siktberg)

Le Petit-Rien
(Rondeau)

Francois Couperin
(arranged for guitar
by Stephen C. Siktberg)

6th = D

(♩ = 145)

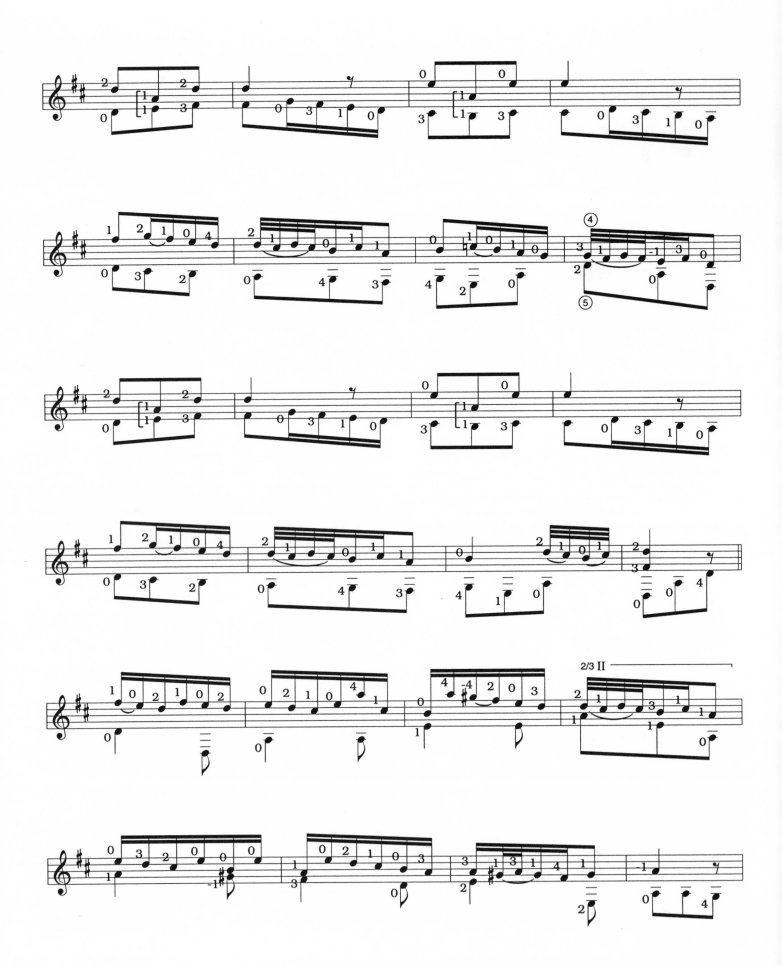

30

31

Le Trophie

Francois Couperin
(arranged for guitar
by Stephen C. Siktberg)

6th = D

La Flore

Capo 3rd fret
3rd = F♯

Francois Couperin
(arranged for guitar
by Stephen C. Siktberg)

Gracefully
(♪ = 140)

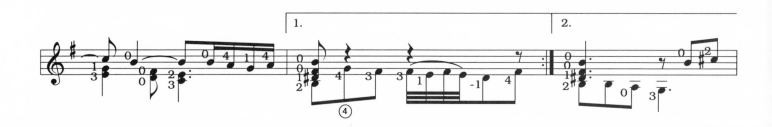

La Morinete

Francois Couperin
(arranged for guitar
by Stephen C. Siktberg)

Les Tambourins

Francois Couperin
(arranged for guitar
by Stephen C. Siktberg)

La Badine

(Rondeau)

Francois Couperin
(arranged for guitar
by Stephen C. Siktberg)

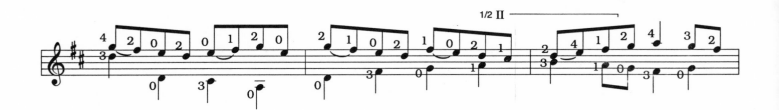

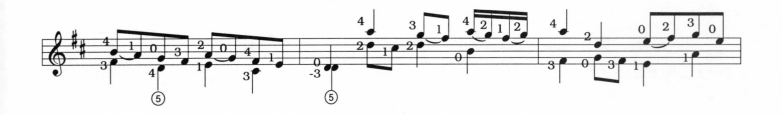

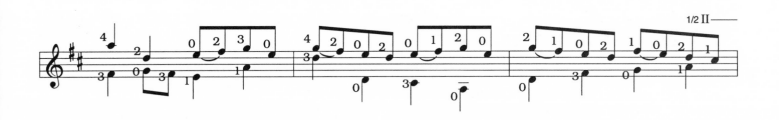

Les Bacchanales

Francois Couperin
(arranged for guitar
by Stephen C. Siktberg)

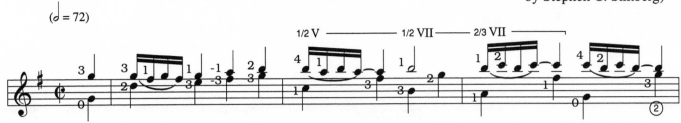

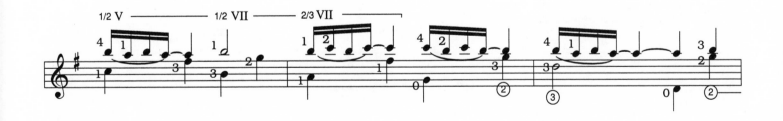

44

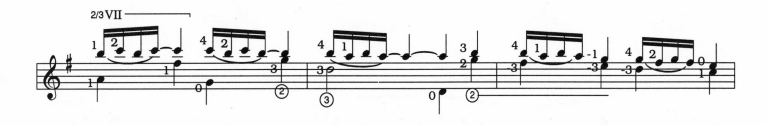

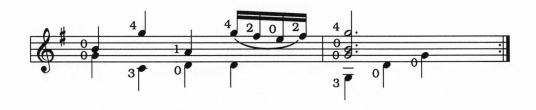

La Bourbonnoise

(Gavotte)

Francois Couperin
(arranged for guitar
by Stephen C. Siktberg)

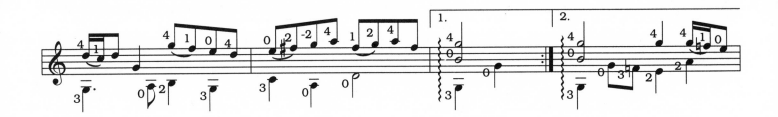

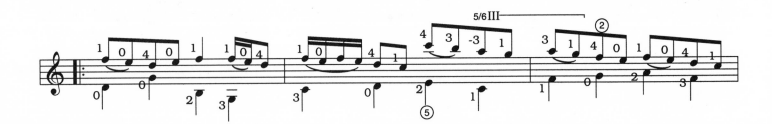

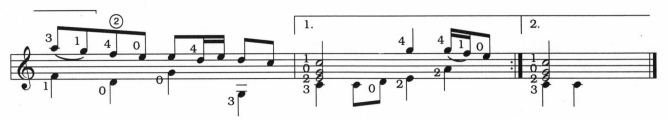

Menuet en Rondeau

Jean-Philippe Rameau
(arranged for guitar
by Stephen C. Siktberg)

Menuet

Jean-Philippe Rameau
(Arranged for Guitar
by Stephen C. Siktberg)

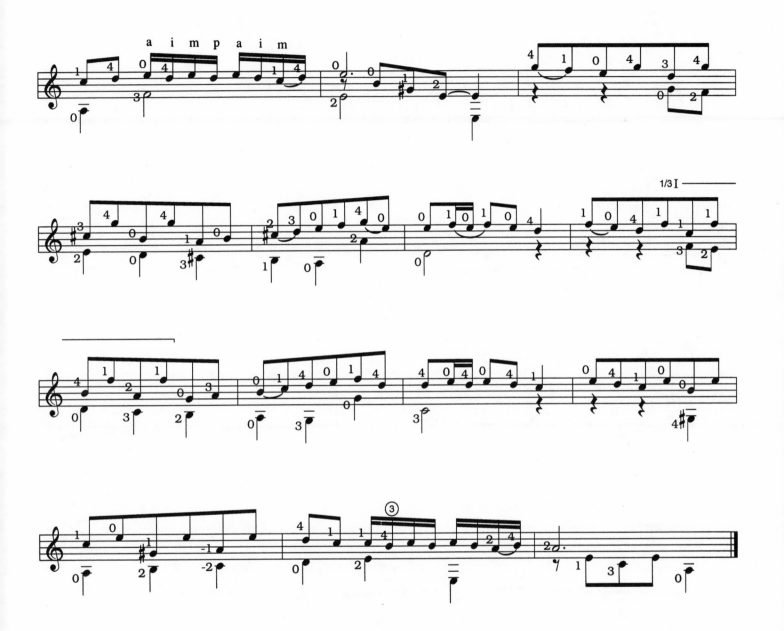

Sarabande 1

Jean-Philippe Rameau
(arranged for guitar
by Stephen C. Siktberg)

Sarabande 2

Jean-Philippe Rameau
(arranged for guitar
by Stephen C. Siktberg)

Sarabande 1 da capo

Gavotte en Rondeau

Jean-Philippe Rameau
(arranged for guitar
by Stephen C. Siktberg)

53

Les Tendres Plaintes
(Rondeau)

Jean-Philippe Rameau
(arranged for guitar
by Stephen C. Siktberg)

55

Menuet 1

Jean-Philippe Rameau
(arranged for guitar
by Stephen C. Siktberg)

Menuet 2

Jean-Philippe Rameau
(arranged for guitar
by Stephen C. Siktberg)

Menuet 1 da capo

*This page has been
left blank to avoid
awkward page turns*

Sonata in G
(K431)

Domenico Scarlatti
(arranged for guitar
by Stephen C. Siktberg)

Sonata in D minor
(K434)

6th = D

Domenico Scarlatti
(arranged for guitar
by Stephen C. Siktberg)

63

64

Sonata in D
(K414)

Domenico Scarlatti
(arranged for guitar
by Stephen C. Siktberg)

6th = D

67

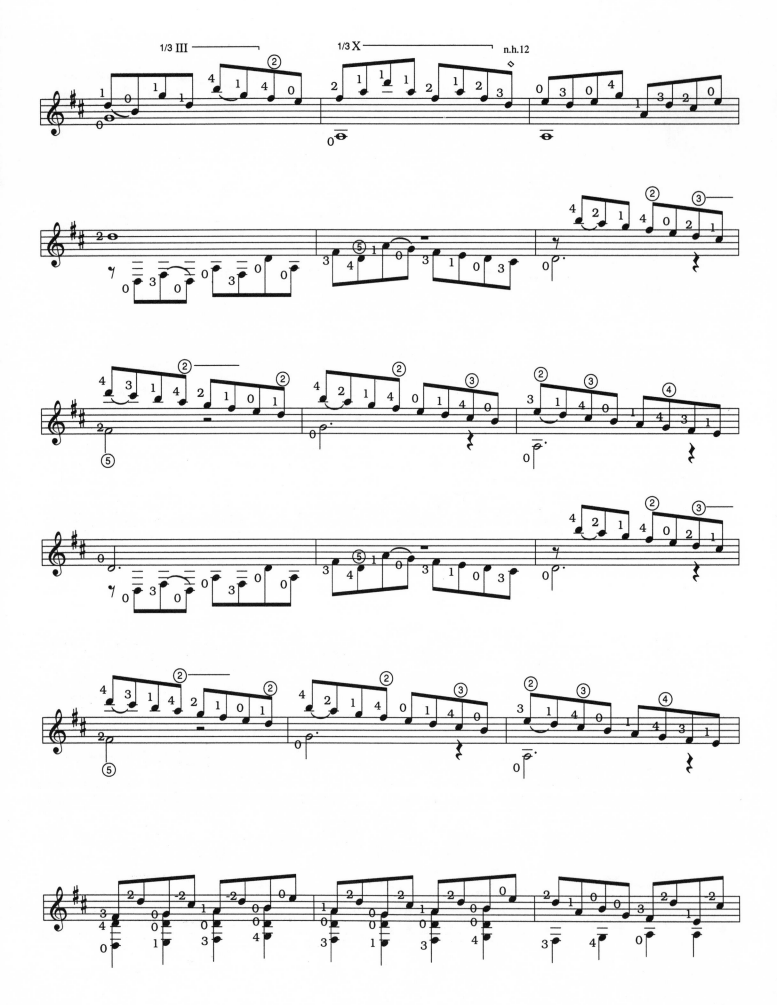

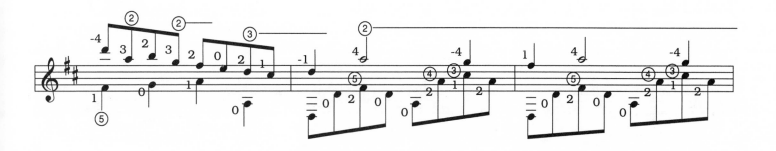

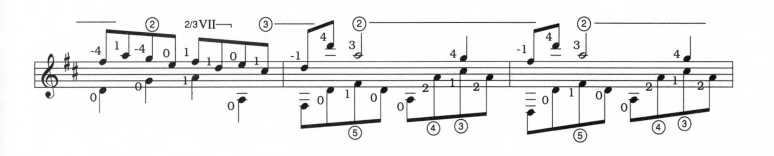

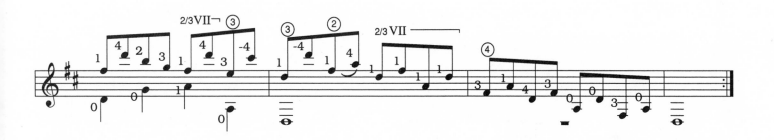

71

Sonata in A
(K428)

Domenico Scarlatti
(arranged for guitar
by Stephen C. Siktberg)

3rd = F♯

(♩ = 104)

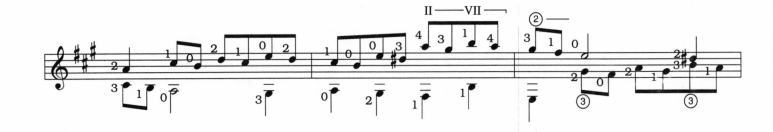

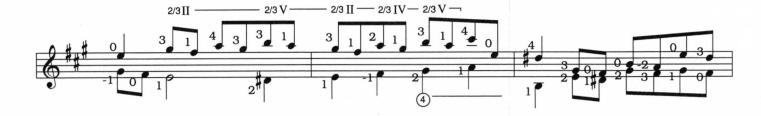

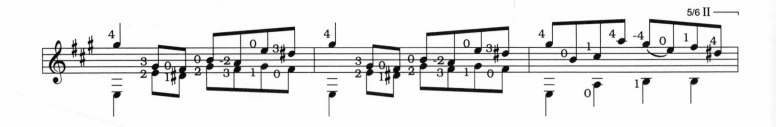

73

Fantasia in Em

George Philip Telemann
(arranged for guitar
by Stephen C. Siktberg)

Tempo di Minuetto

(♪ = 100)

Fantasia in D

George Philip Telemann
(arranged for guitar
by Stephen C. Siktberg)

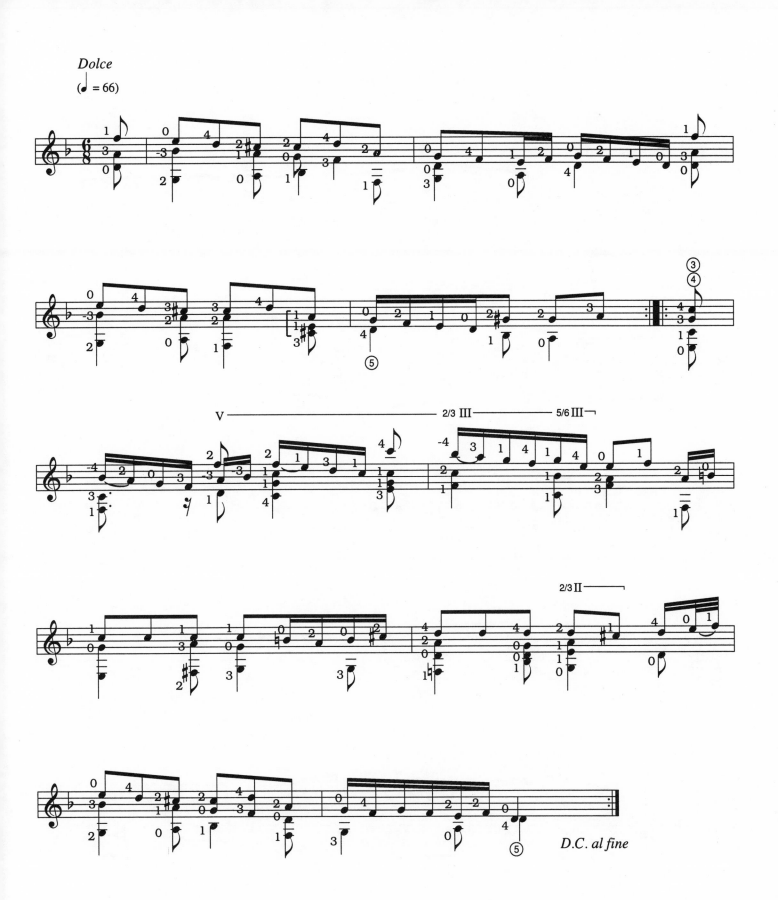

Fantasia in D

George Philip Telemann
(arranged for guitar
by Stephen C. Siktberg)

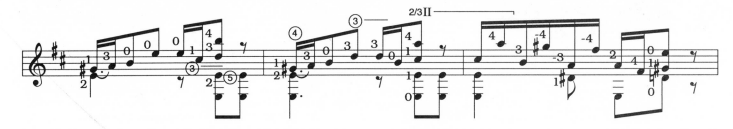

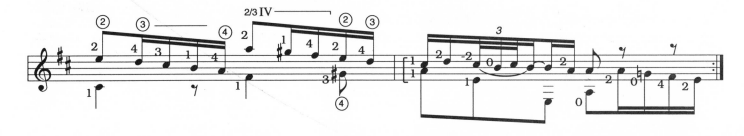

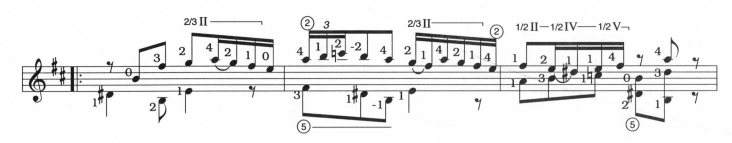

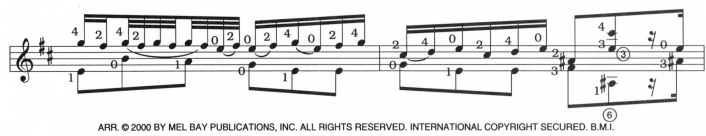

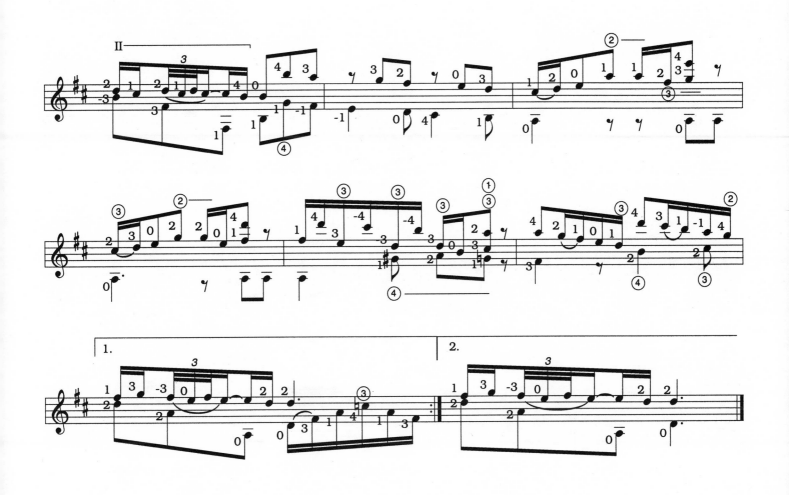

83

Fantasia in Dm

George Philip Telemann
(arranged for guitar
by Stephen C. Siktberg)

Fantasia in Am

George Philip Telemann
(arranged for guitar
by Stephen C. Siktberg)

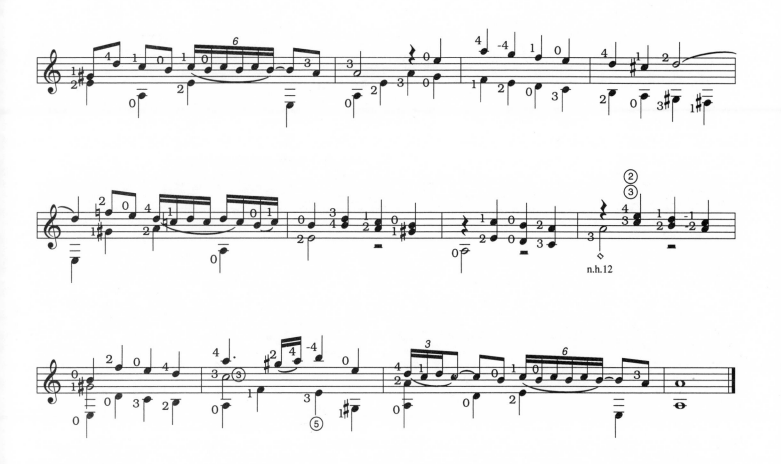

Fantasia in C

George Philip Telemann
(arranged for guitar
by Stephen C. Siktberg)

Tenderly
(♩ = 92)

89

91

Fantasia in Em

George Philip Telemann
(arranged for guitar
by Stephen C. Siktberg)

94

95

Sonatina in C

George Friedrich Handel
(arranged for guitar
by Stephen C. Siktberg)

Allemande

George Friedrich Handel
(arranged for guitar
by Stephen C. Siktberg)

Sarabande
(with variations)

George Friedrich Handel
(arranged for guitar
by Stephen C. Siktberg)

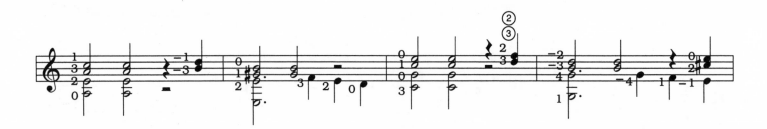

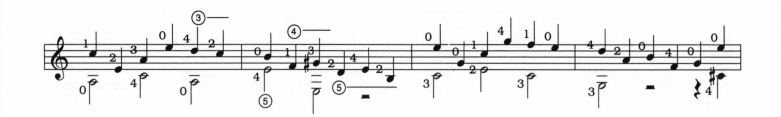

*This page has been
left blank to avoid
awkward page turns*

Allegro
(from Great Suite #7 for Harpsichord)

George Friedrich Handel
(arranged for guitar
by Stephen C. Siktberg)

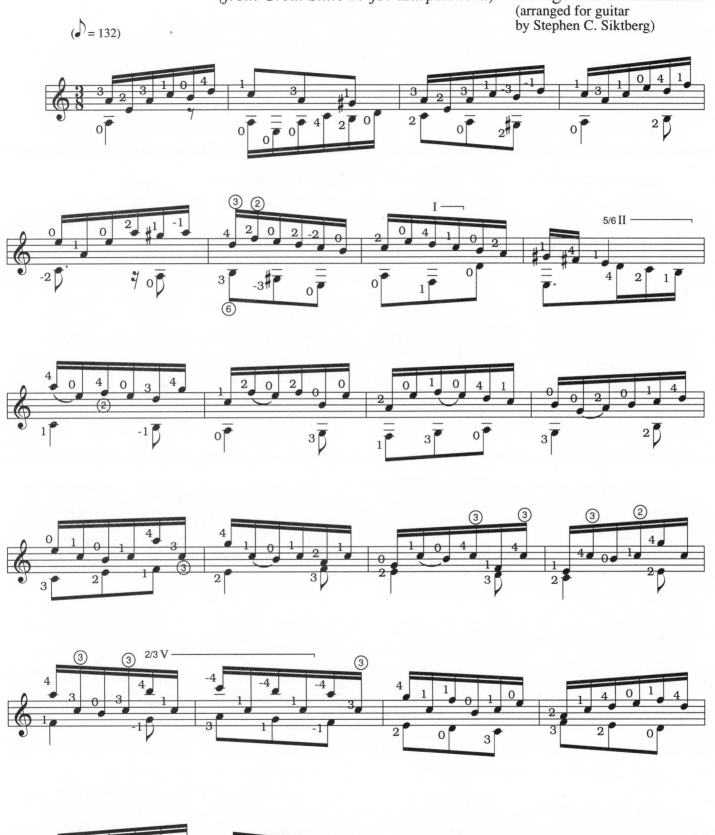

105

Sarabande

(from Great Suite #7 for Harpsichord)

George Friedrich Handel
(arranged for guitar
by Stephen C. Siktberg)

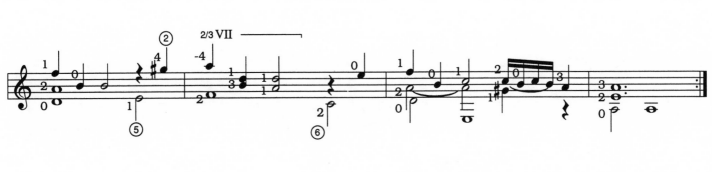

Passacaille
(from Great Suite #7 for Harpsichord)

George Friedrich Handel
(arranged for guitar
by Stephen C. Siktberg)

110

111

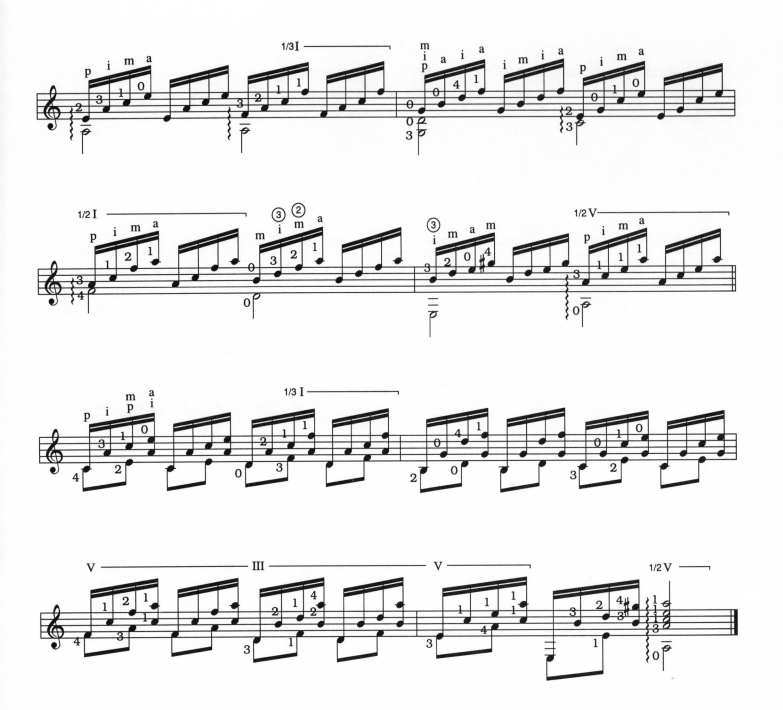

Allegro

(from Partita in G major for Harpsichord)

George Friedrich Handel
(arranged for guitar
by Stephen C. Siktberg)

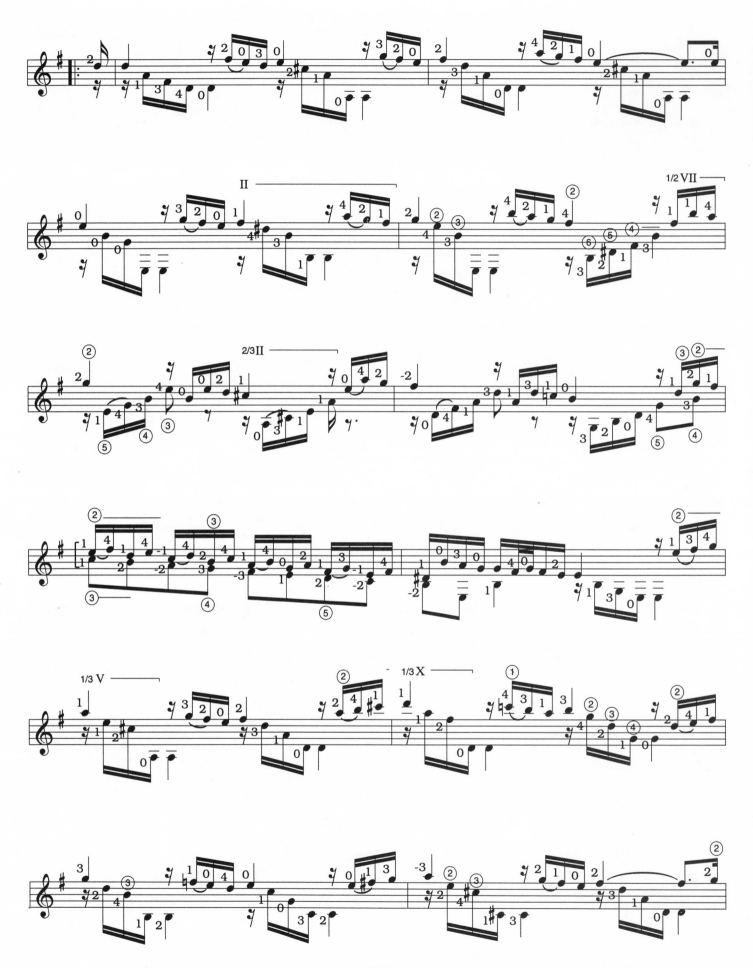

114

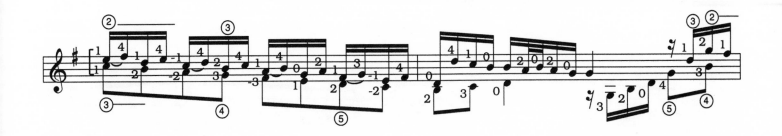

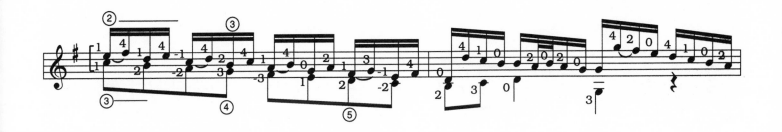

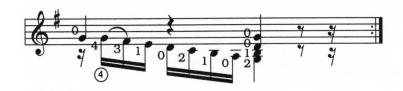

Courante
(from Partita in G major for Harpsichord)

George Friedrich Handel
(arranged for guitar
by Stephen C. Siktberg)

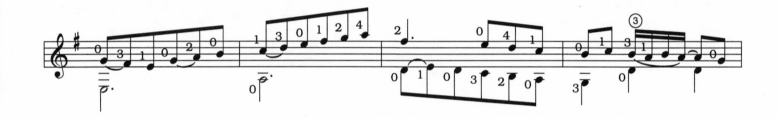

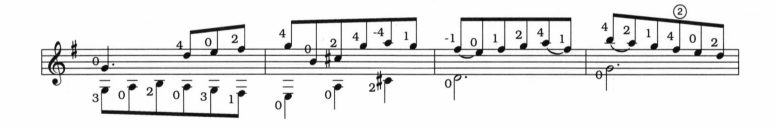

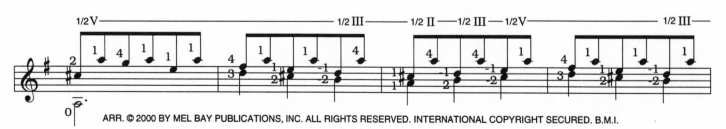

117

118

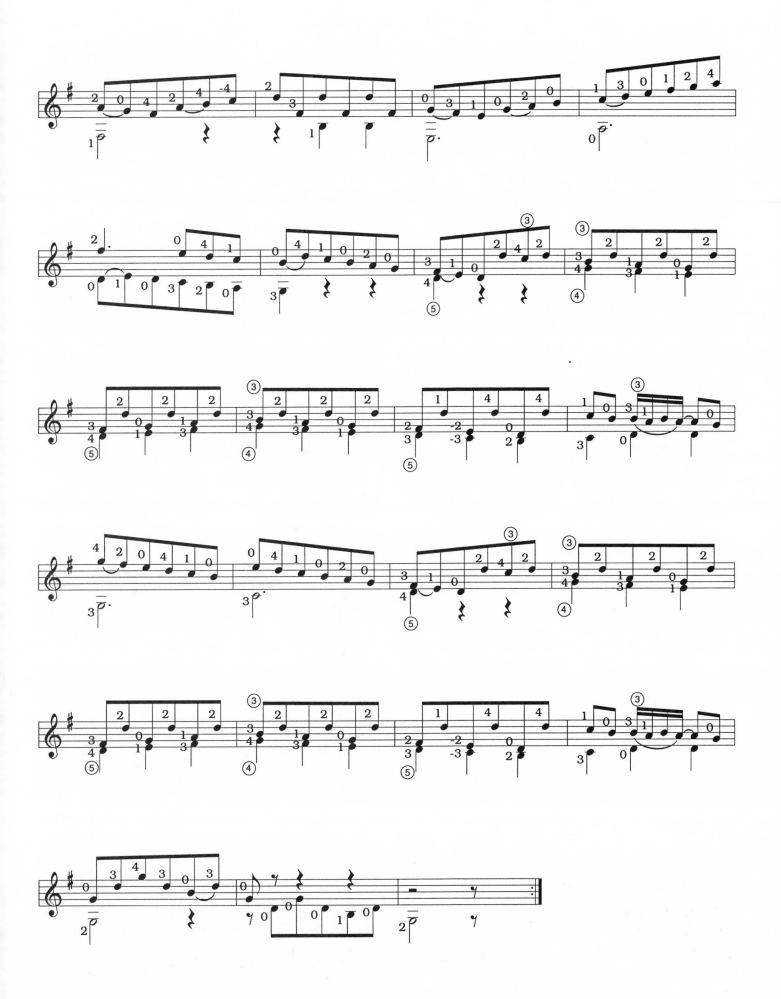

119

Sonata in C

Capo 3rd fret

George Friedrich Handel
(arranged for guitar
by Stephen C. Siktberg)

(♪ = 144)

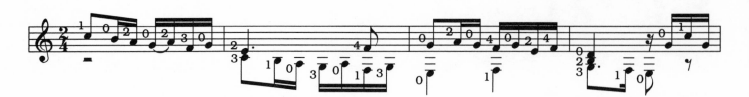

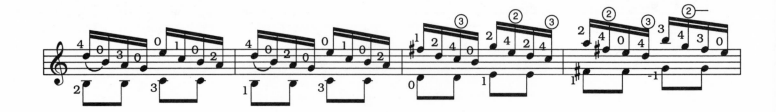

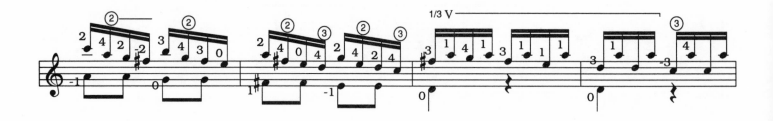

Prelude
(from Suite #1 for Violoncello)

J. S. Bach
(arranged for guitar
by Stephen C. Siktberg)

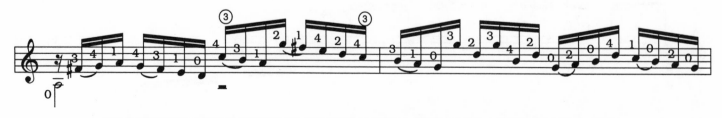

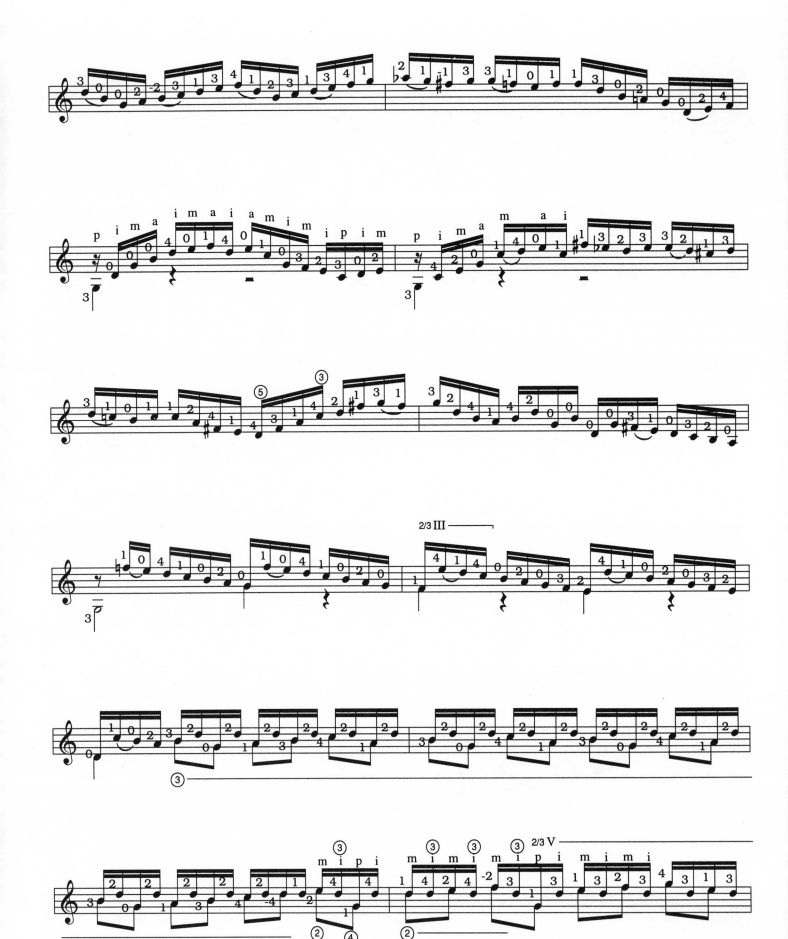

126

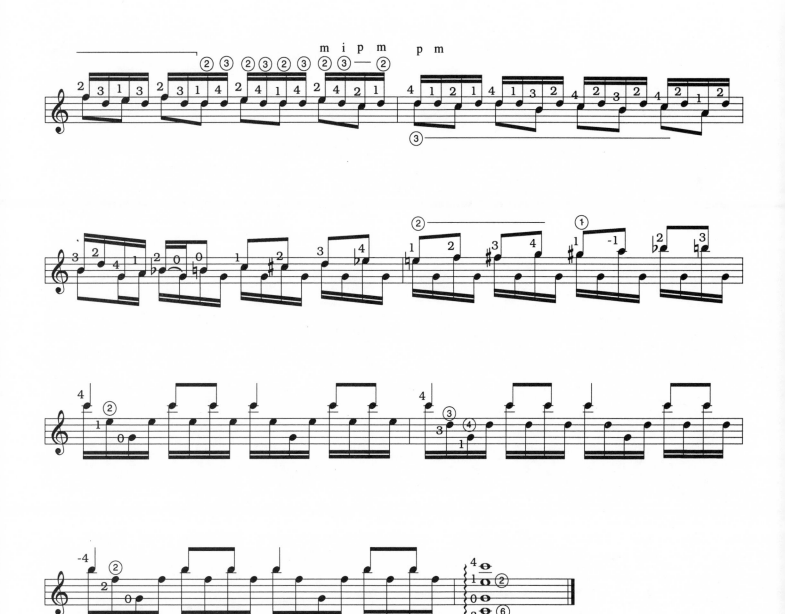

Menuet 1
(from Suite #1 for Violoncello)

J. S. Bach
(arranged for guitar
by Stephen C. Siktberg)

(♩ = 110)

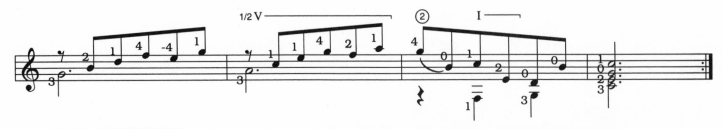

Menuet 2
(from Suite #1 for Violoncello)

J. S. Bach
(arranged for guitar
by Stephen C. Siktberg)

Menuet 1 da capo

Gigue

(from Suite #1 for Violoncello)

J. S. Bach
(arranged for guitar
by Stephen C. Siktberg)

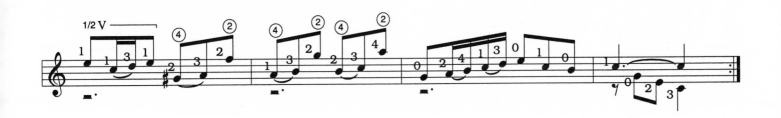

Gavotte 1
(from Suite #6 for Violoncello)

J. S. Bach
(arranged for guitar
by Stephen C. Siktberg)

Gavotte 2
(from Suite #6 for Violoncello)

J. S. Bach
(arranged for guitar
by Stephen C. Siktberg)

Gavotte 1 da capo

Gavotte en Rondeau
(from Partita #3 for Violin)

J. S. Bach
(arranged for guitar
by Stephen C. Siktberg)

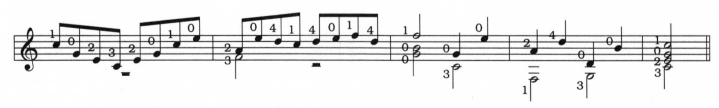

135

137

Menuet 1
(from Partita #3 for Violin)

J. S. Bach
(arranged for guitar
by Stephen C. Siktberg)

(♩ = 116)

Menuet 2
(from Partita #3 for Violin)

J. S. Bach
(arranged for guitar
by Stephen C. Siktberg)

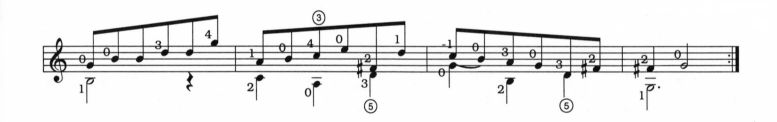

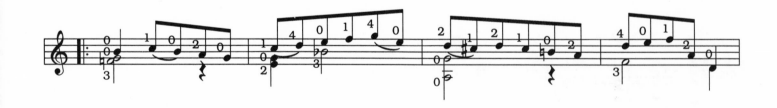

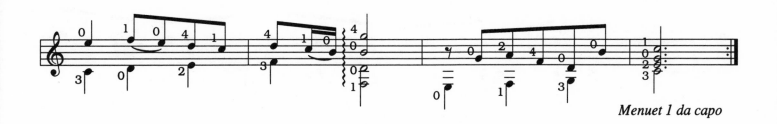

Menuet 1 da capo

141

Bourée

(from Partita #3 for Violin)

J. S. Bach
(arranged for guitar
by Stephen C. Siktberg)

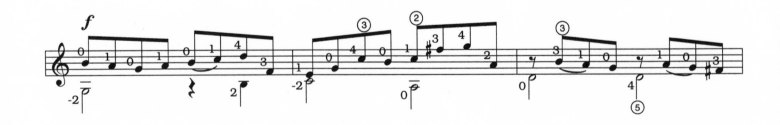

Sarabande & Double

(from Partita #1 for Violin)

J. S. Bach
(arranged for guitar
by Stephen C. Siktberg)

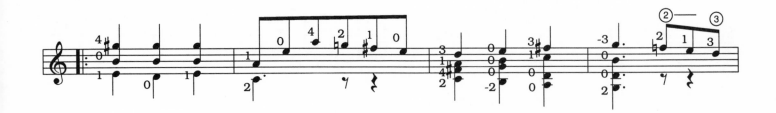

Double

(♩. = 100)

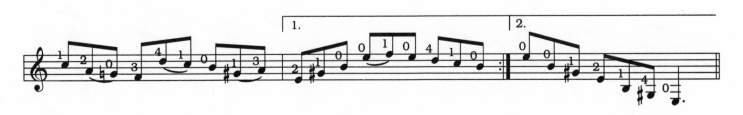

146

Tempo di Bourée
(from Partita #1 for Violin)

J. S. Bach
(arranged for guitar
by Stephen C. Siktberg)

149

150

Fugue in C

Johann Pachelbel
(arranged for guitar
by Stephen C. Siktberg)

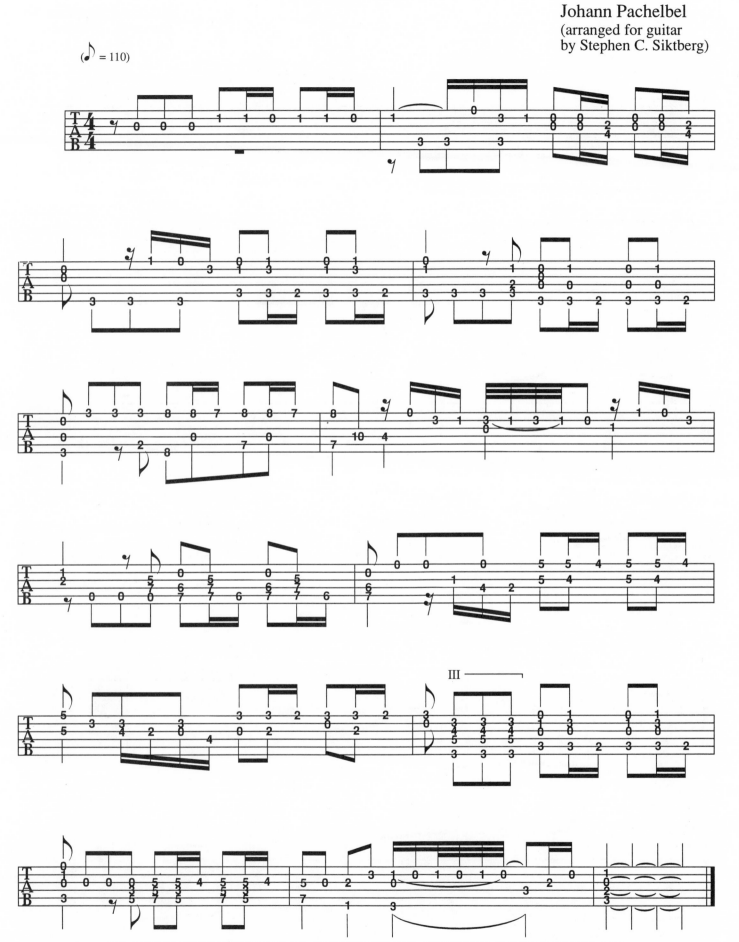

Fugue in G

Johann Pachelbel
(arranged for guitar
by Stephen C. Siktberg)

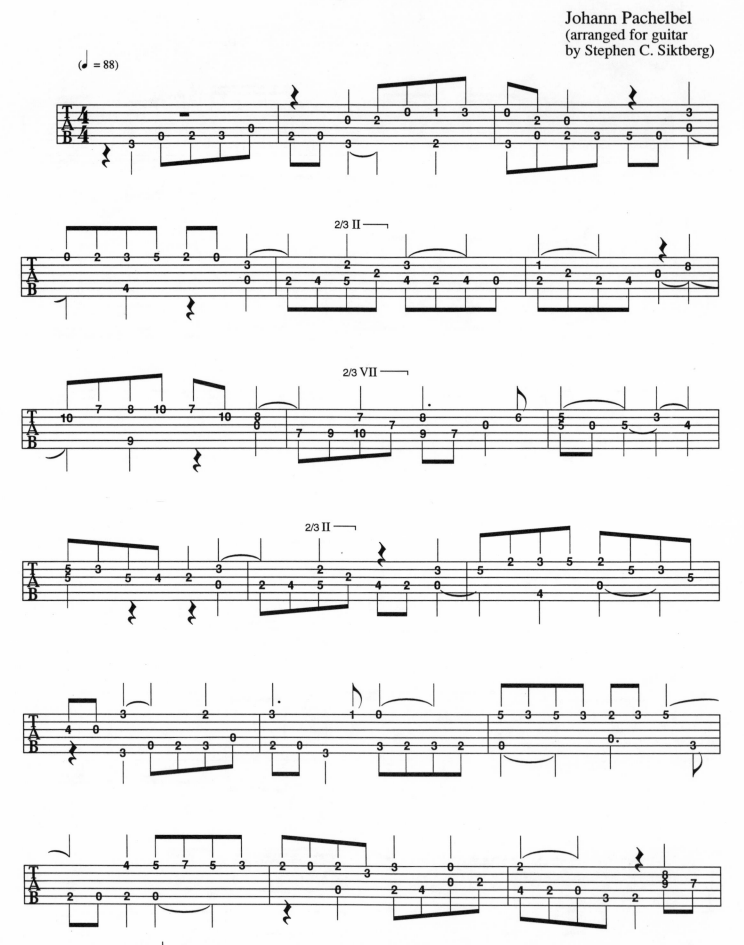

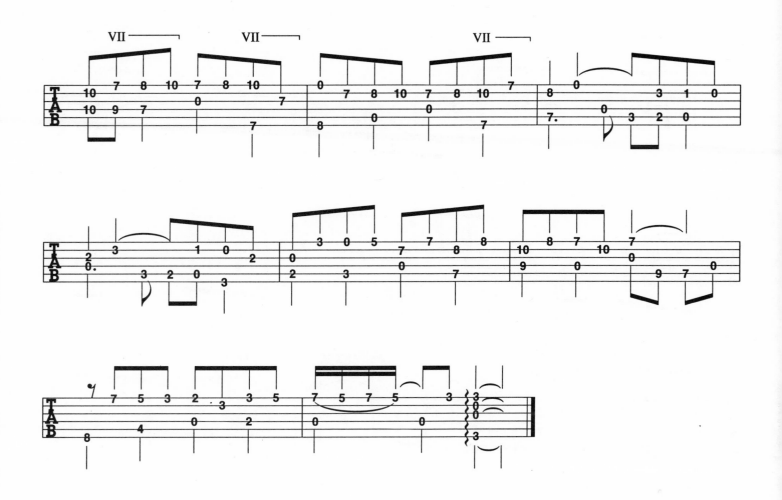

Fugue in G

Johann Pachelbel
(arranged for guitar
by Stephen C. Siktberg)

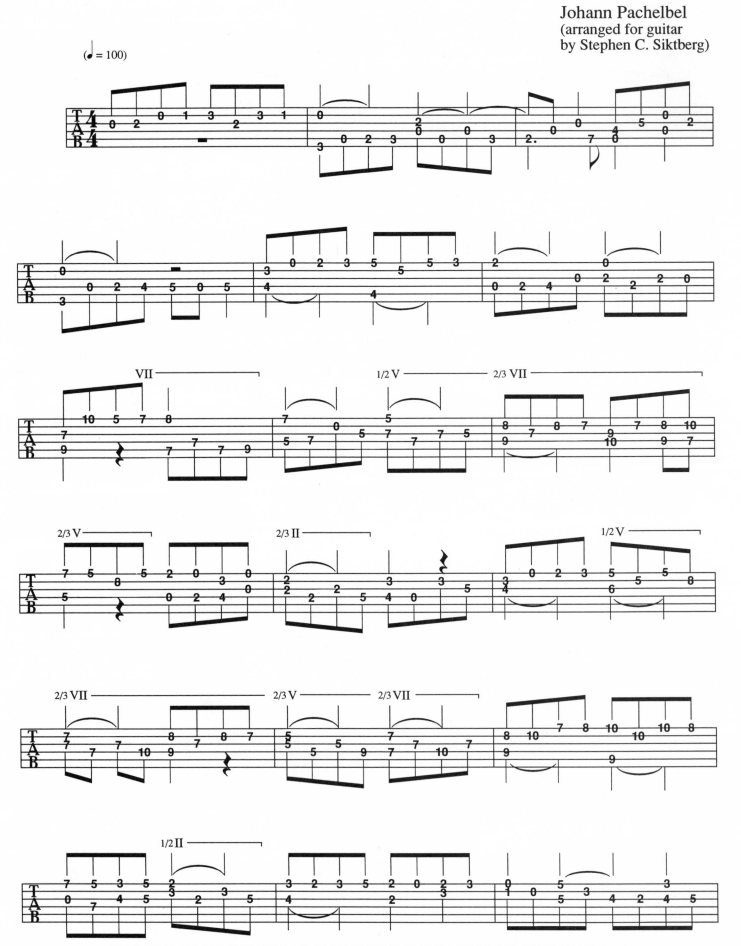

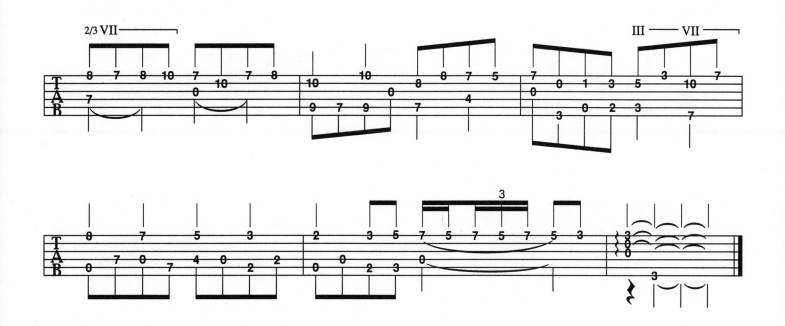

Fugue in Dm

Johann Pachelbel
(arranged for guitar
by Stephen C. Siktberg)

6th = D

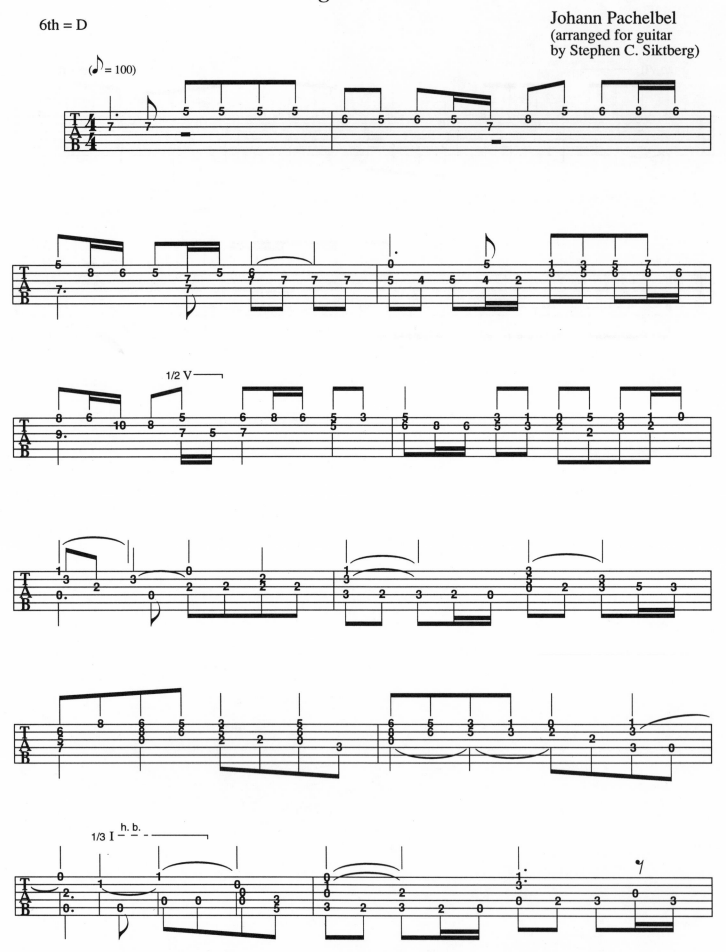

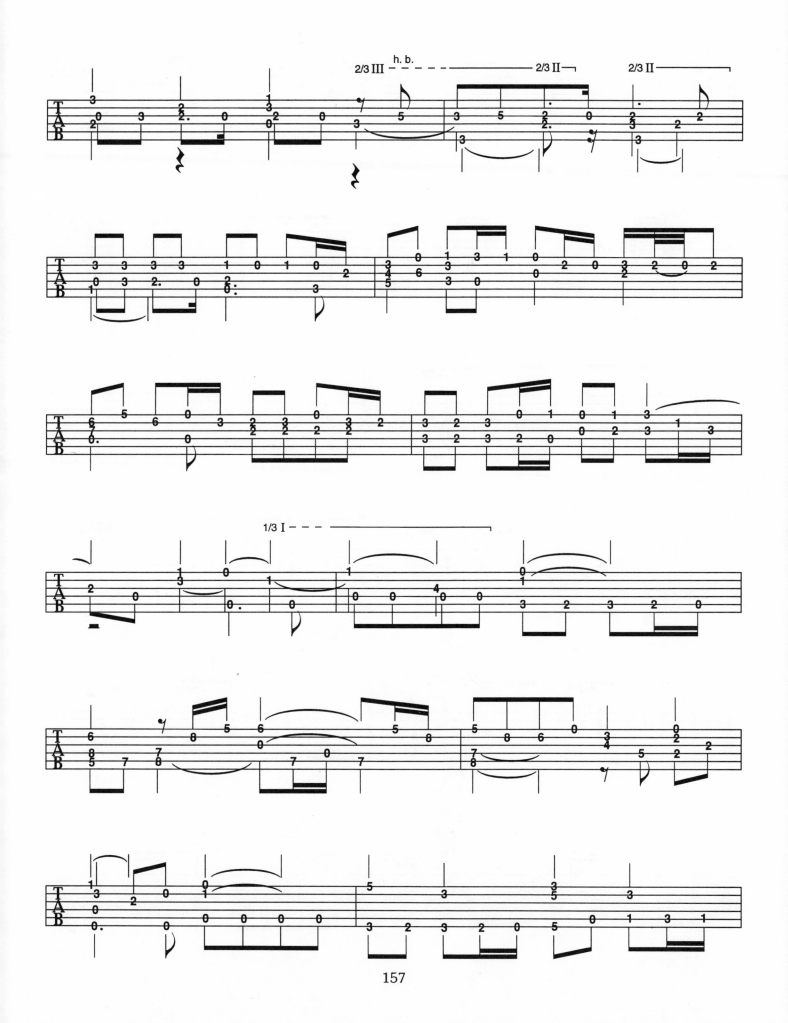

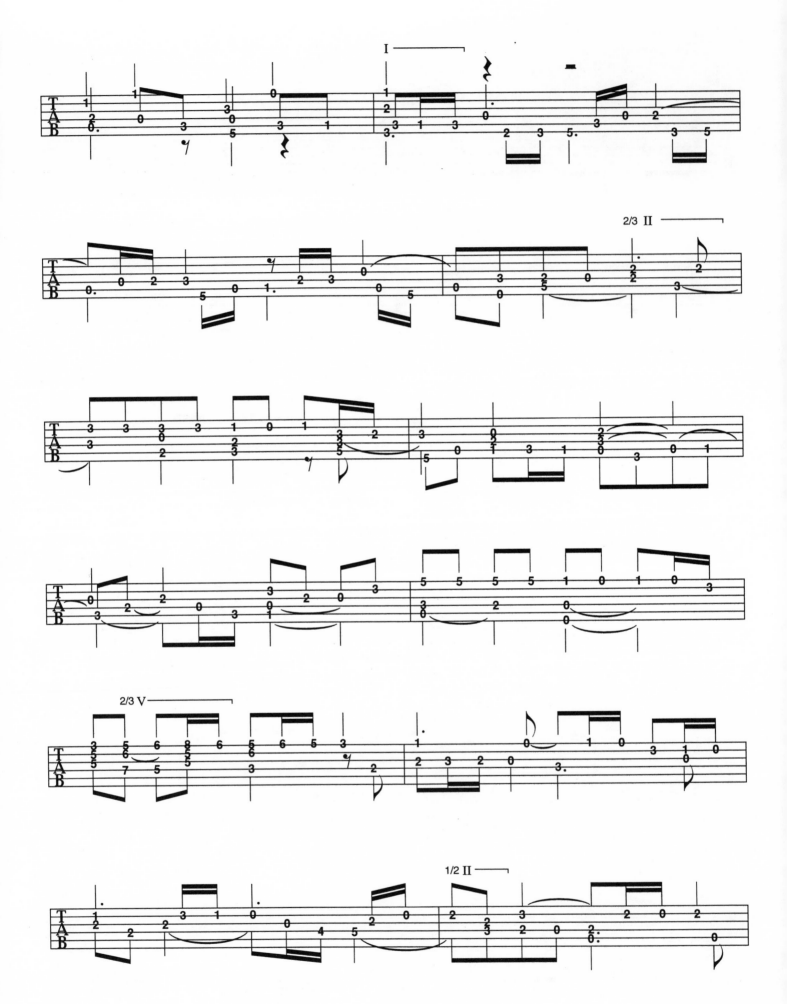

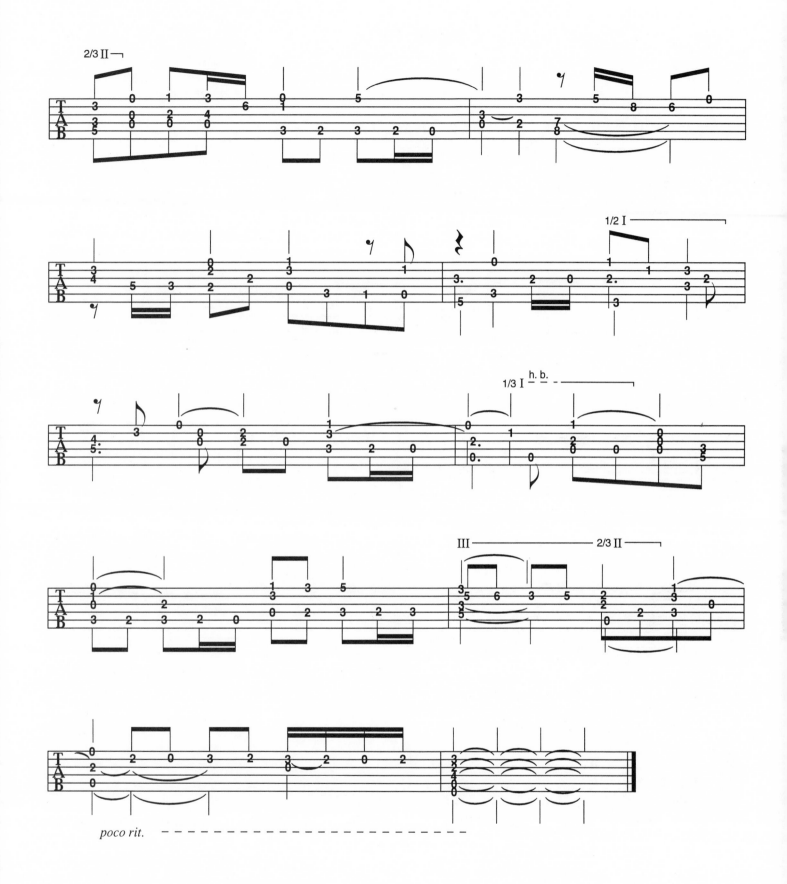

poco rit. –

159

Fugue in D

Johann Pachelbel
(arranged for guitar
by Stephen C. Siktberg)

6th = D

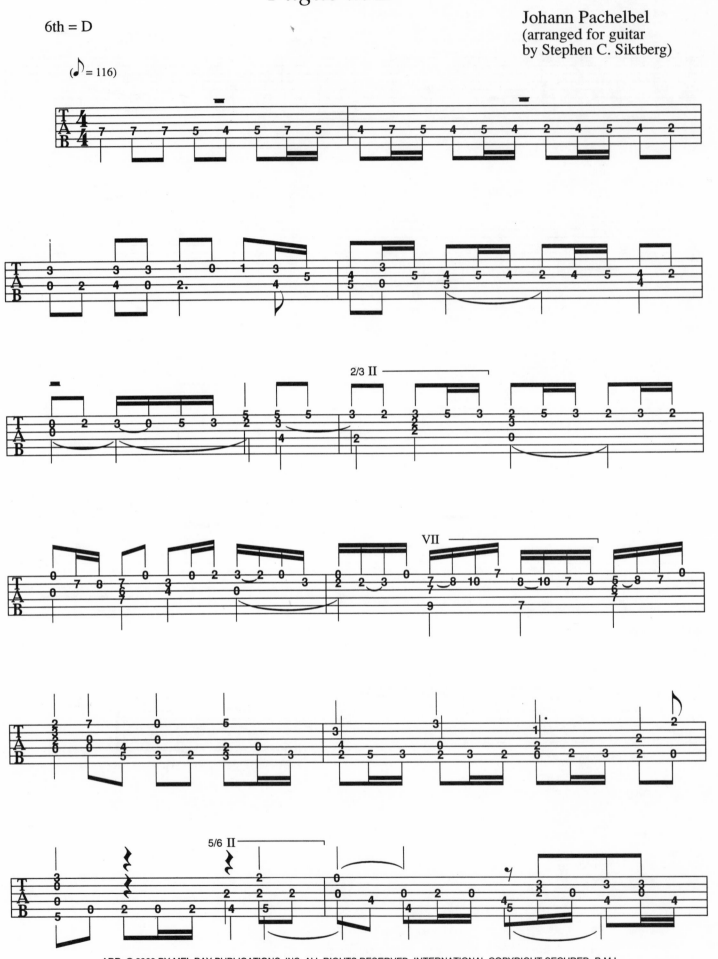

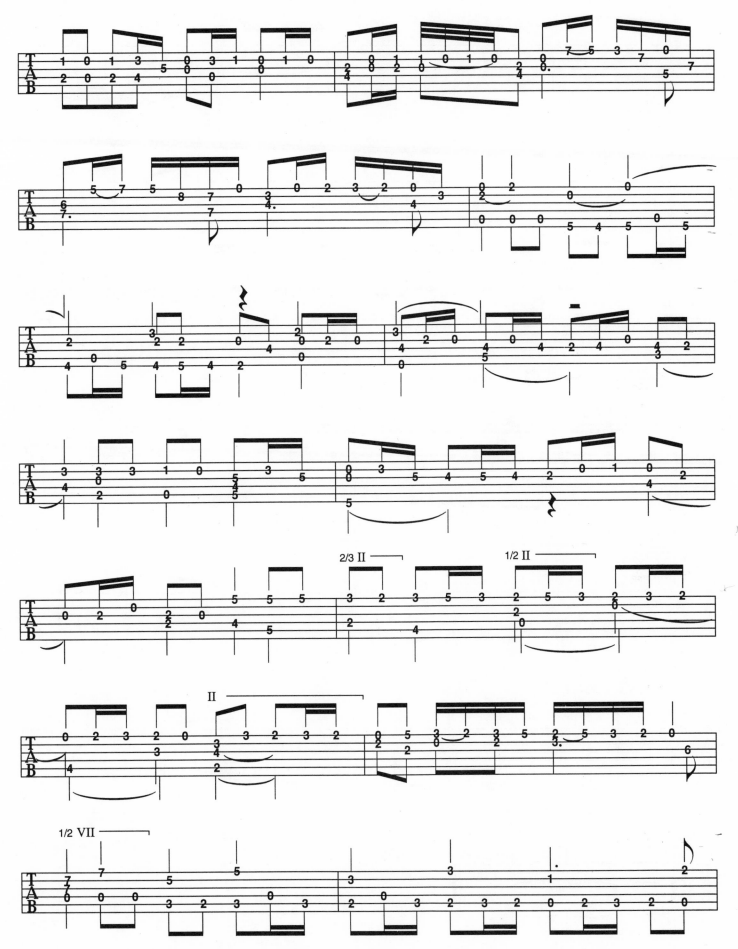

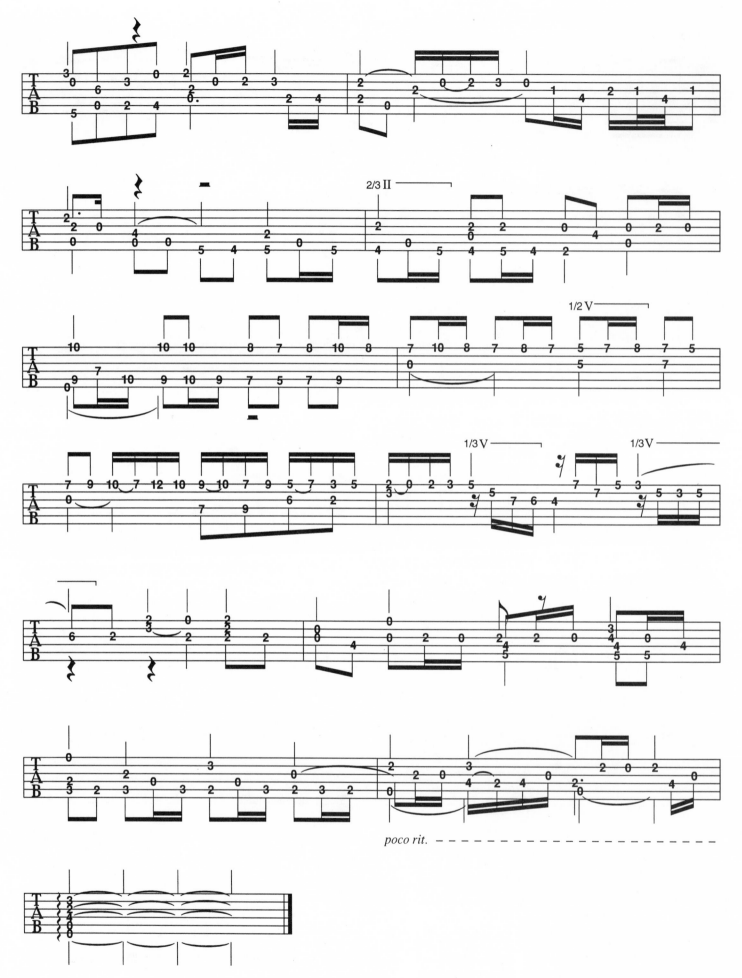

poco rit. –

162

Air in Em

Henry Purcell
(arranged for guitar
by Stephen C. Siktberg)

(♩ = 130)

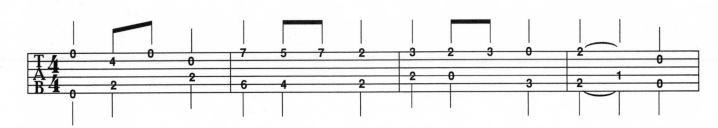

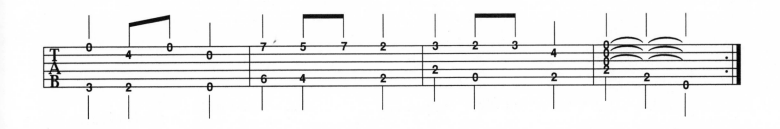

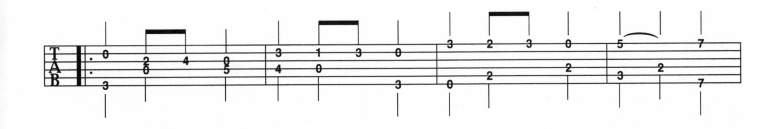

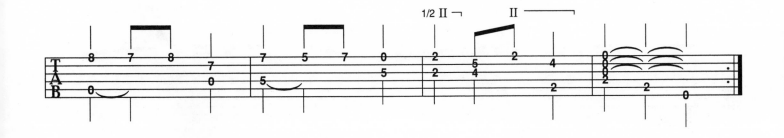

Hornpipe in Em

Henry Purcell
(arranged for guitar
by Stephen C. Siktberg)

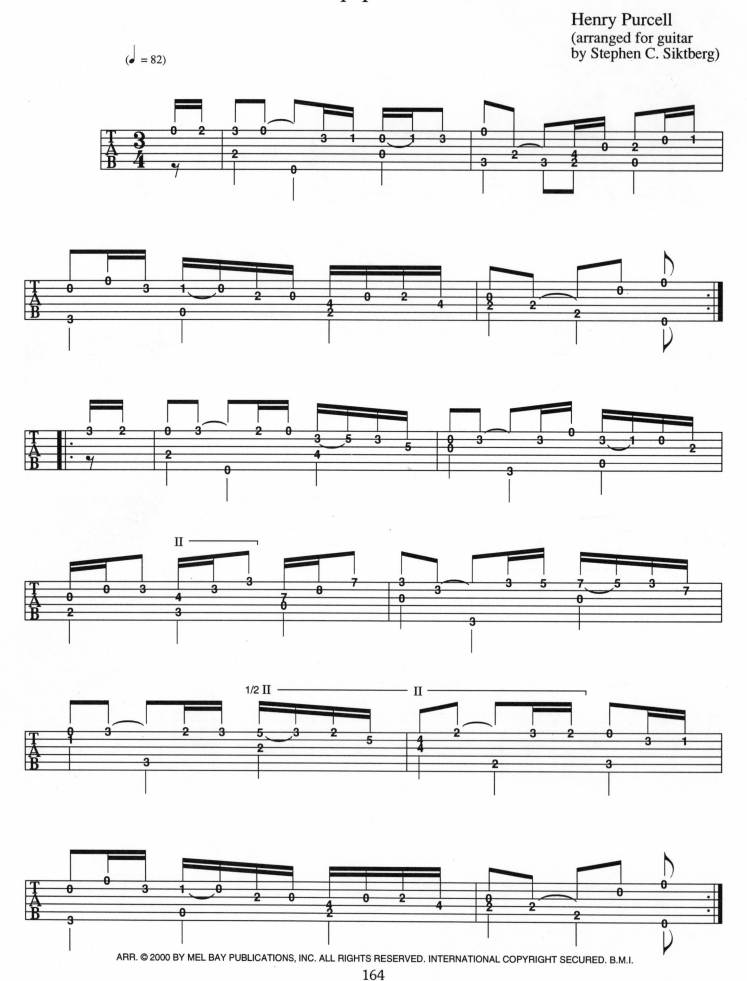

Prelude

Henry Purcell
(arranged for guitar
by Stephen C. Siktberg)

6th = D

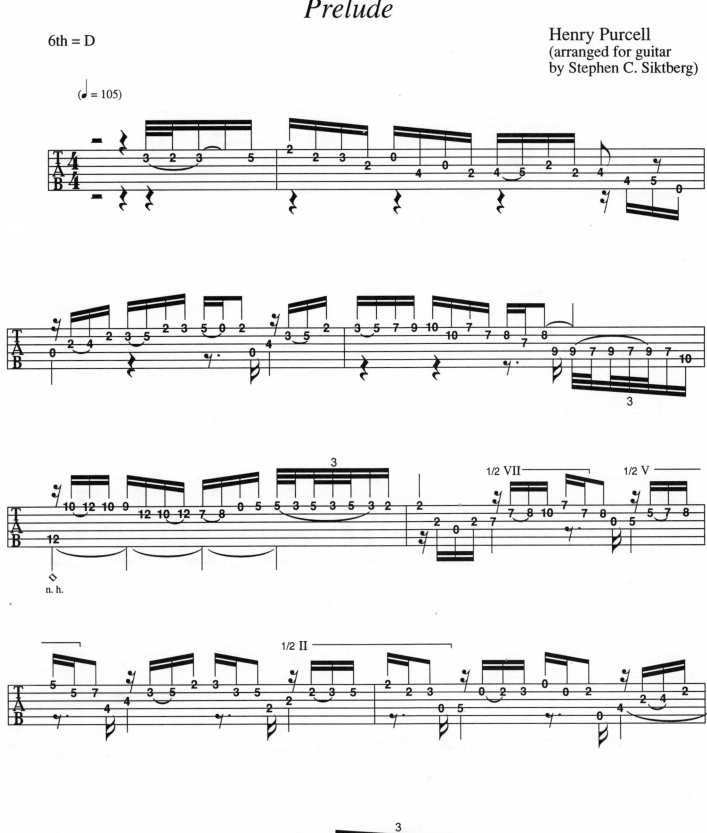

Prelude

Henry Purcell
(arranged for guitar
by Stephen C. Siktberg)

6th = D

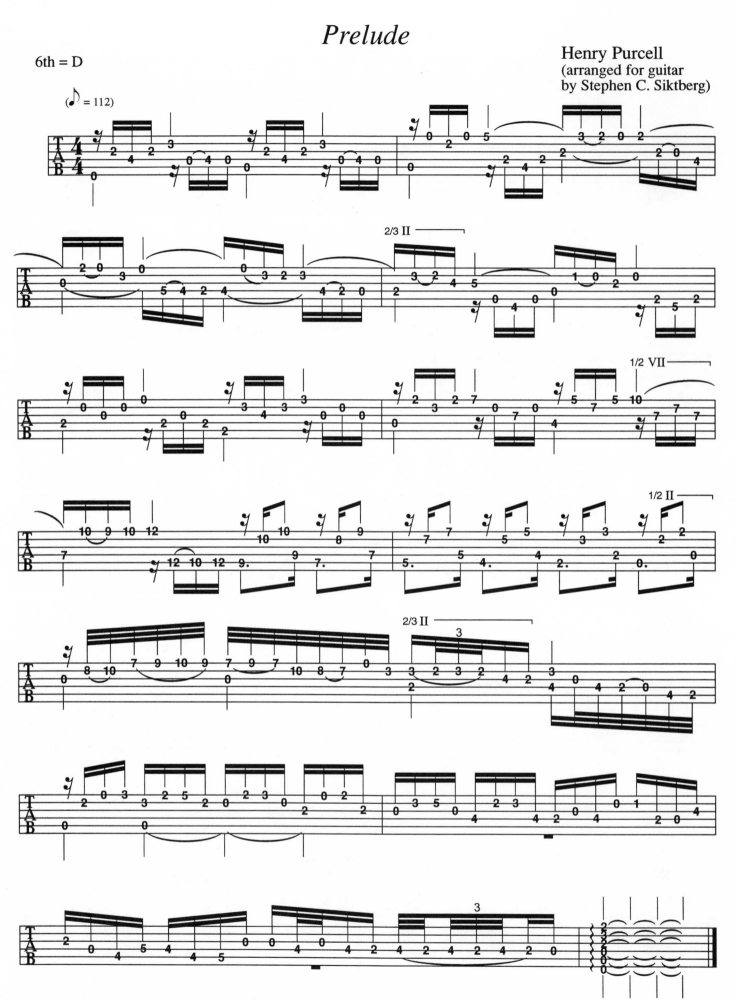

March in D

6th = D

Henry Purcell
(arranged for guitar
by Stephen C. Siktberg)

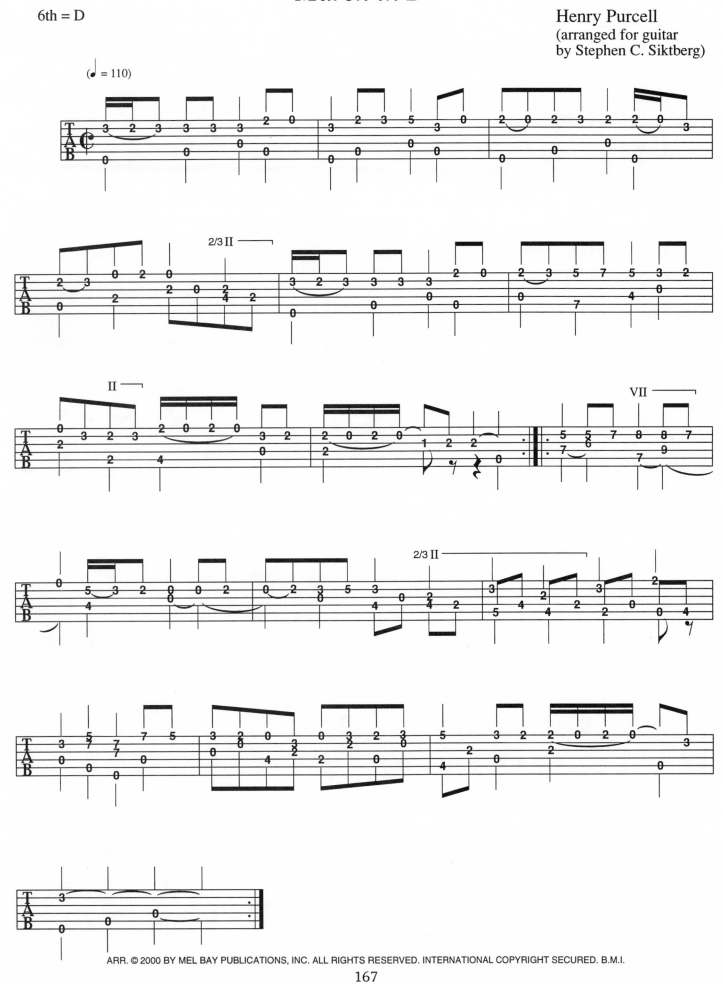

A Ground in G

Henry Purcell
(arranged for guitar
by Stephen C. Siktberg)

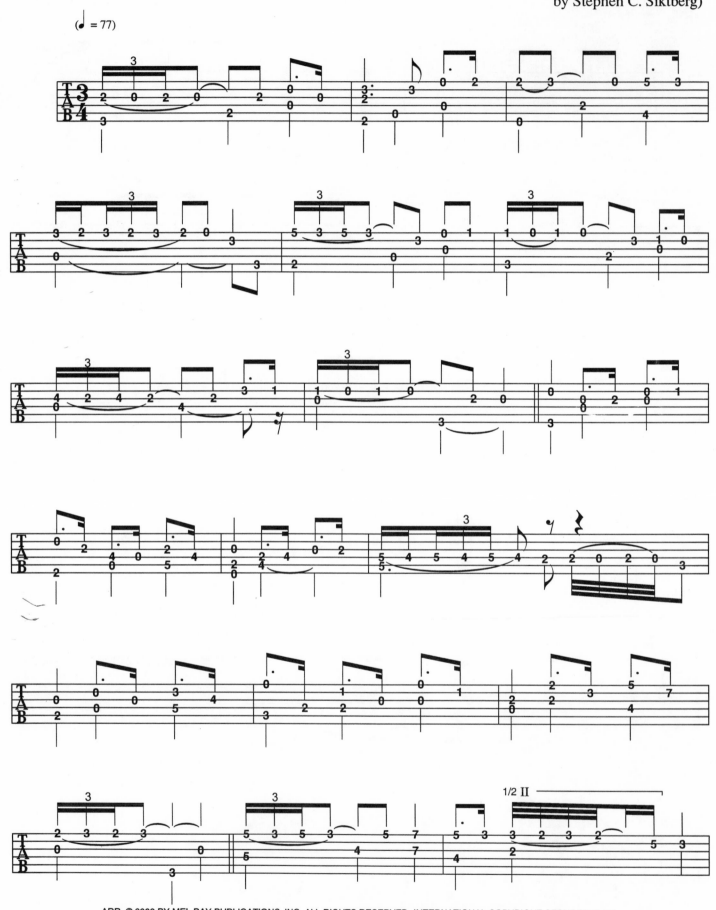

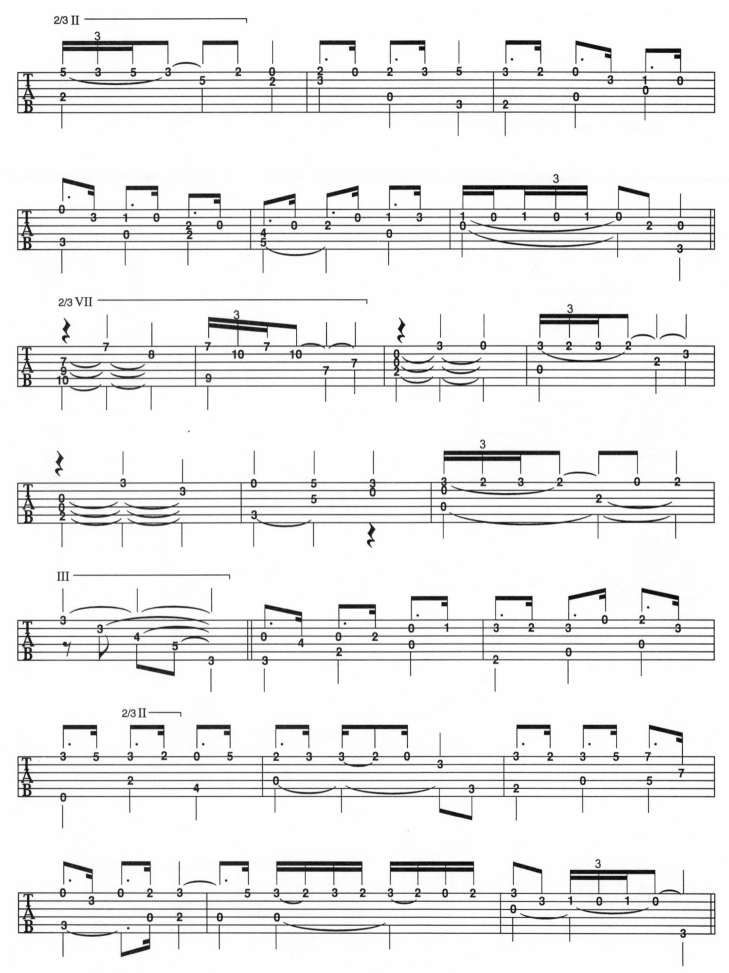

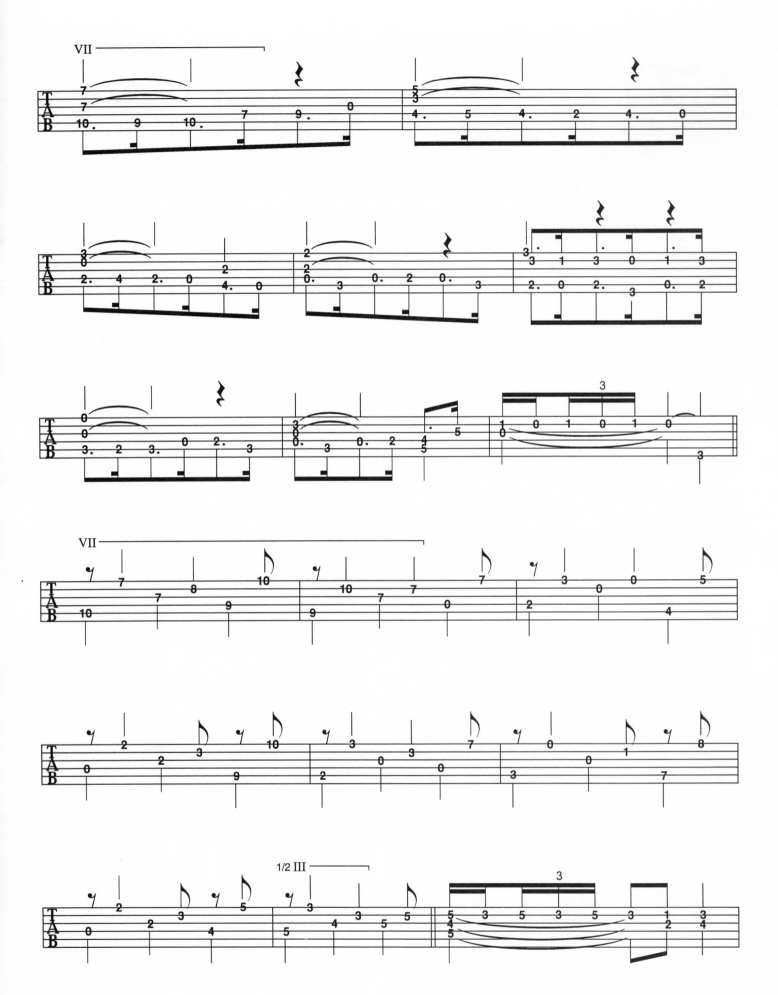

170

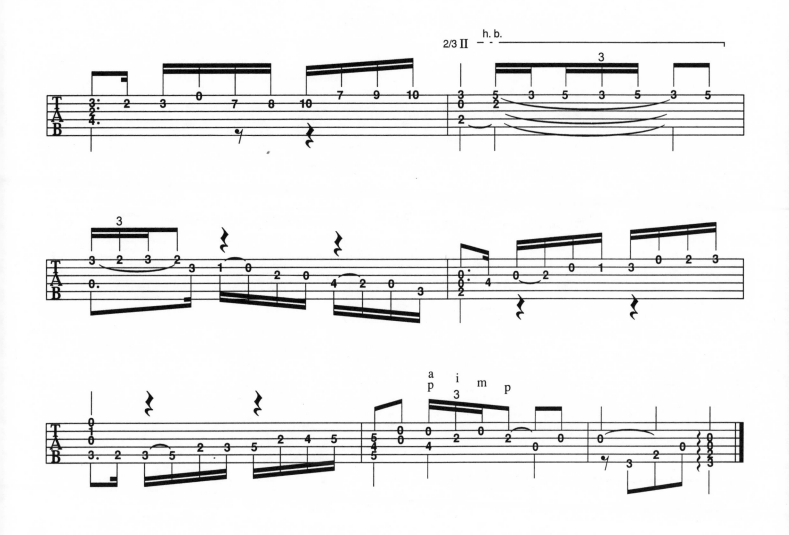

Air in Em

Henry Purcell
(arranged for guitar
by Stephen C. Siktberg)

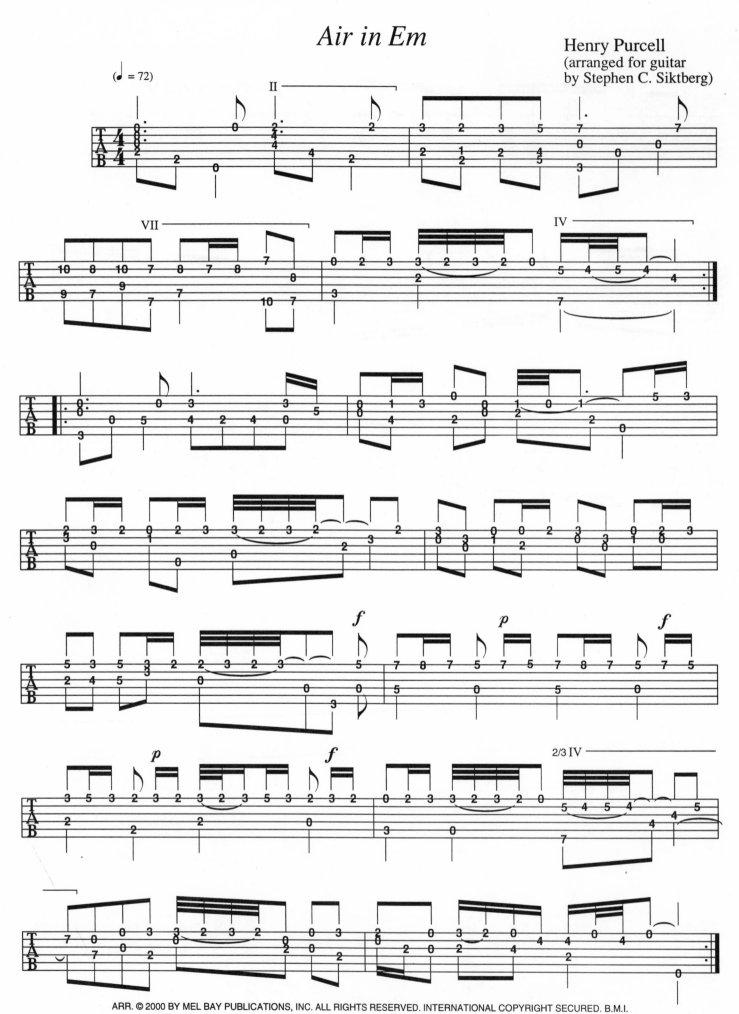

Le Petit-Rien
(Rondeau)

6th = D

Francois Couperin
(arranged for guitar
by Stephen C. Siktberg)

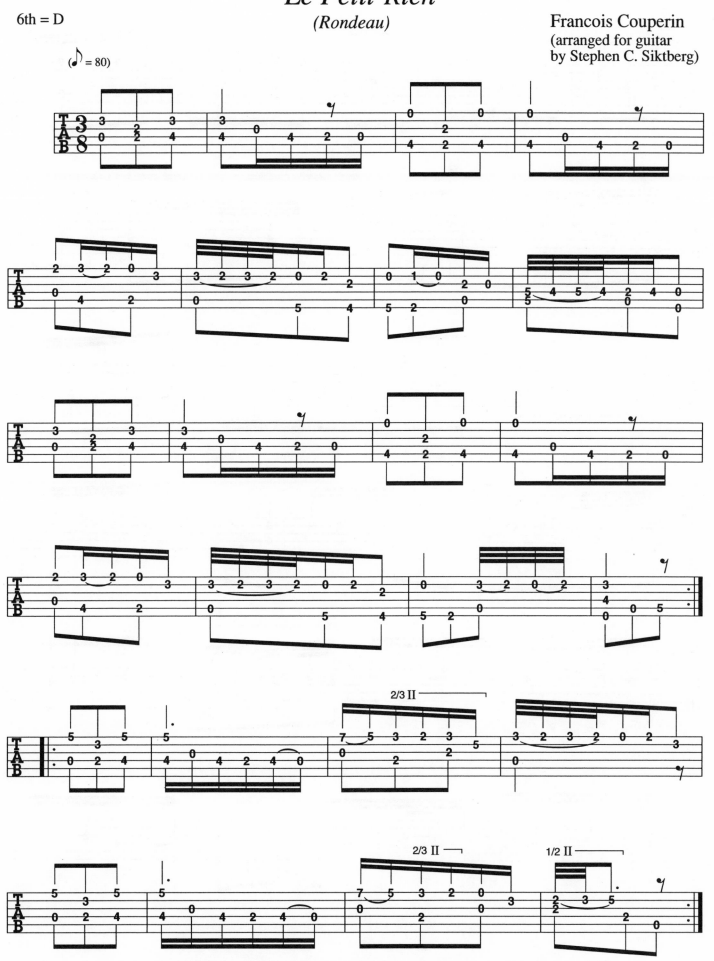

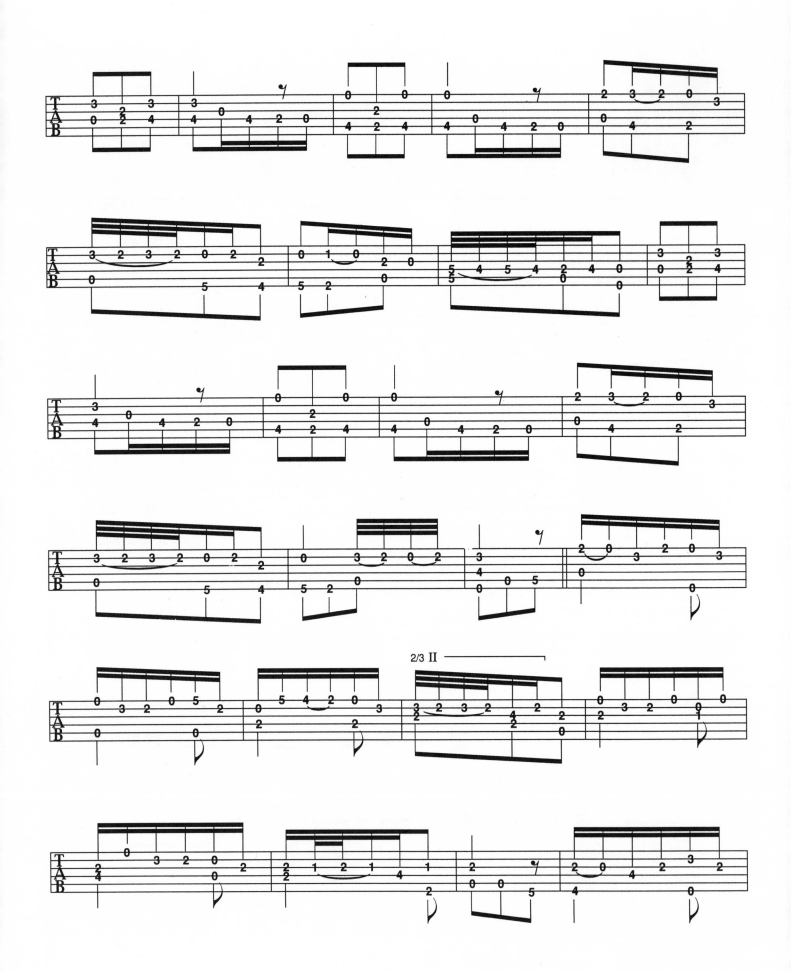

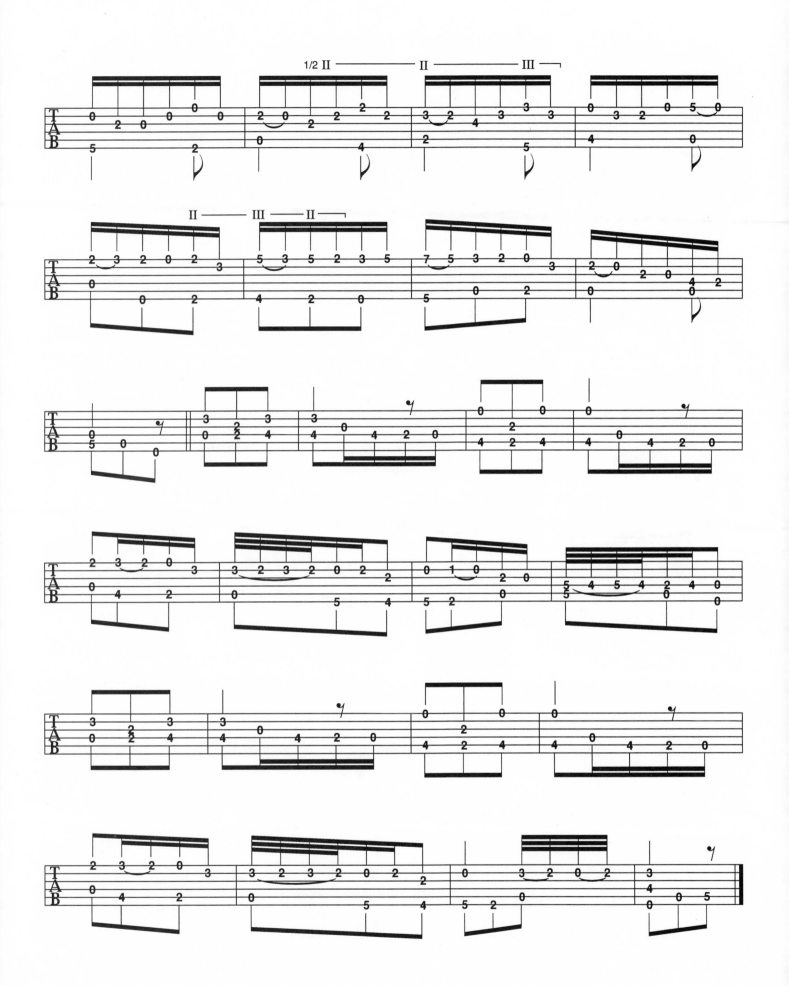

175

Le Trophie

6th = D

Francois Couperin
(arranged for guitar
by Stephen C. Siktberg)

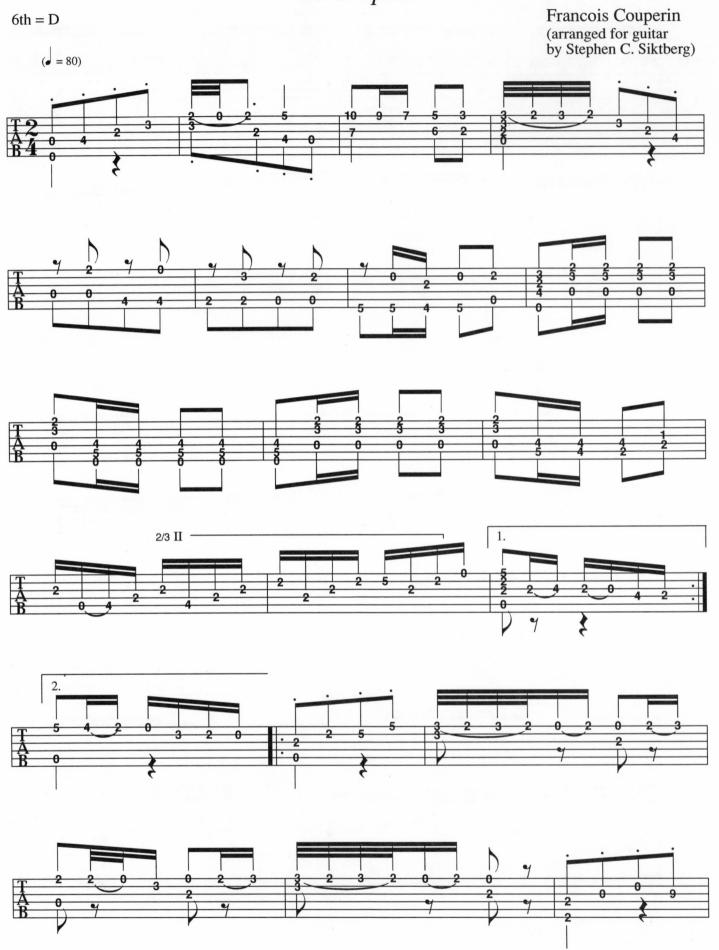

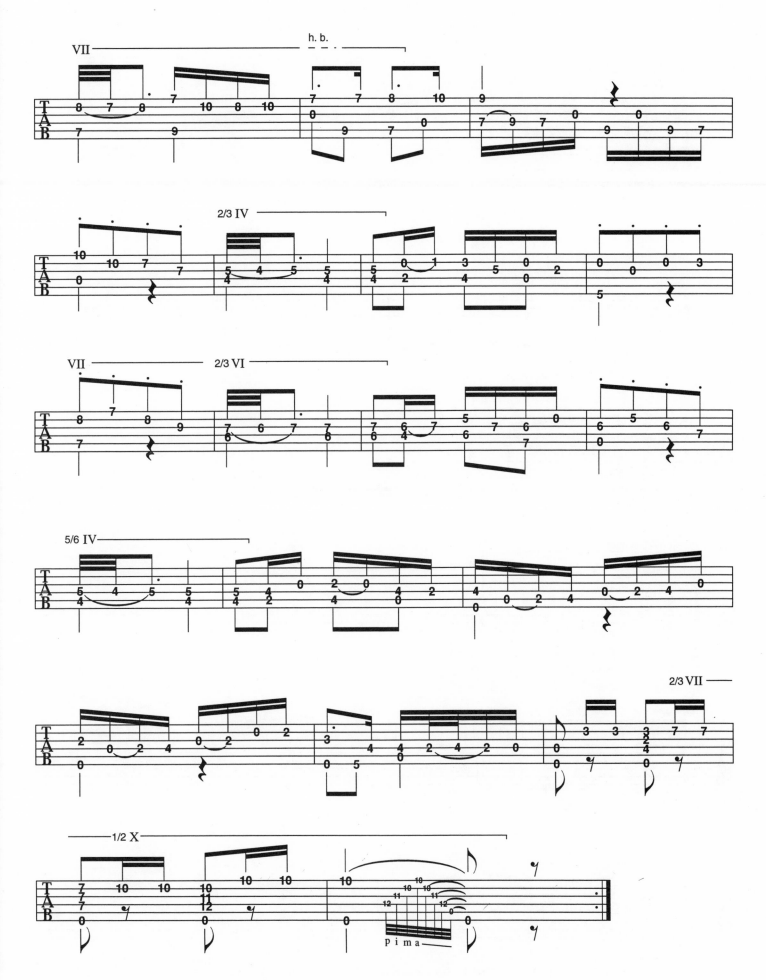

La Flore

Capo 3rd fret
3rd = F#

Francois Couperin
(arranged for guitar
by Stephen C. Siktberg)

Gracefully
(♪ = 140)

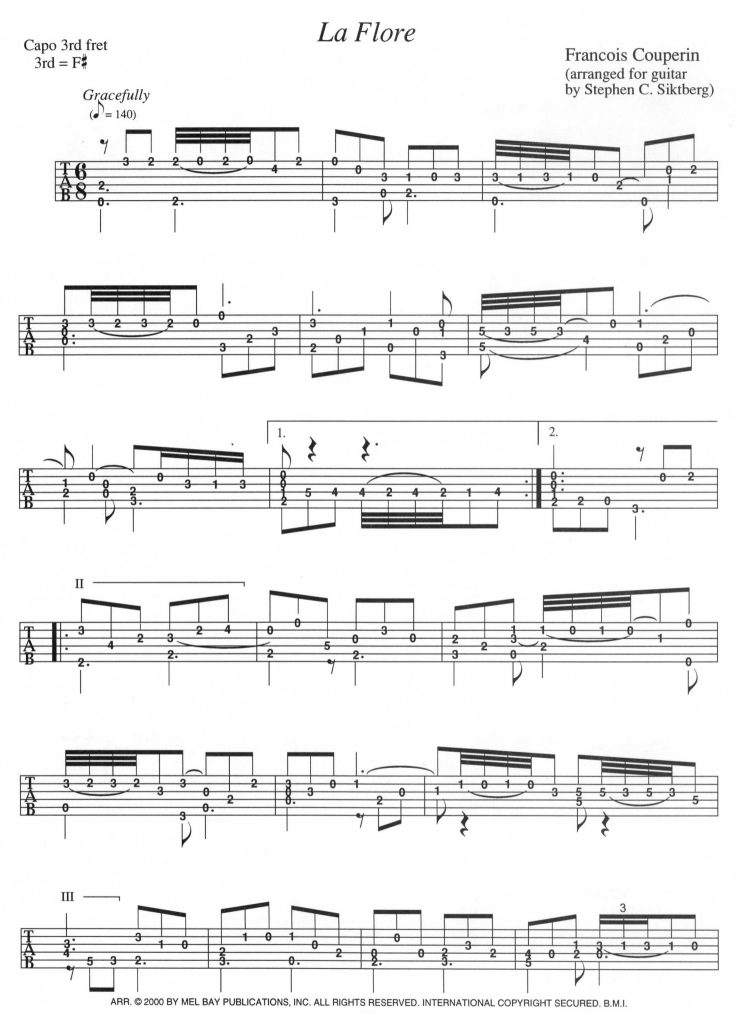

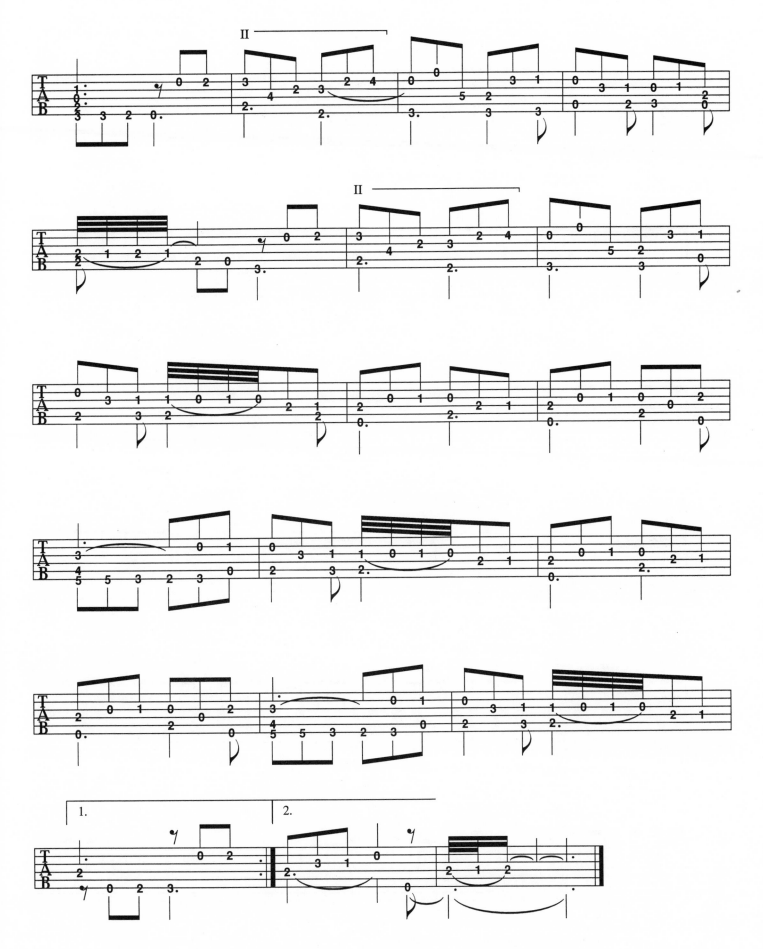

La Morinete

Francois Couperin
(arranged for guitar
by Stephen C. Siktberg)

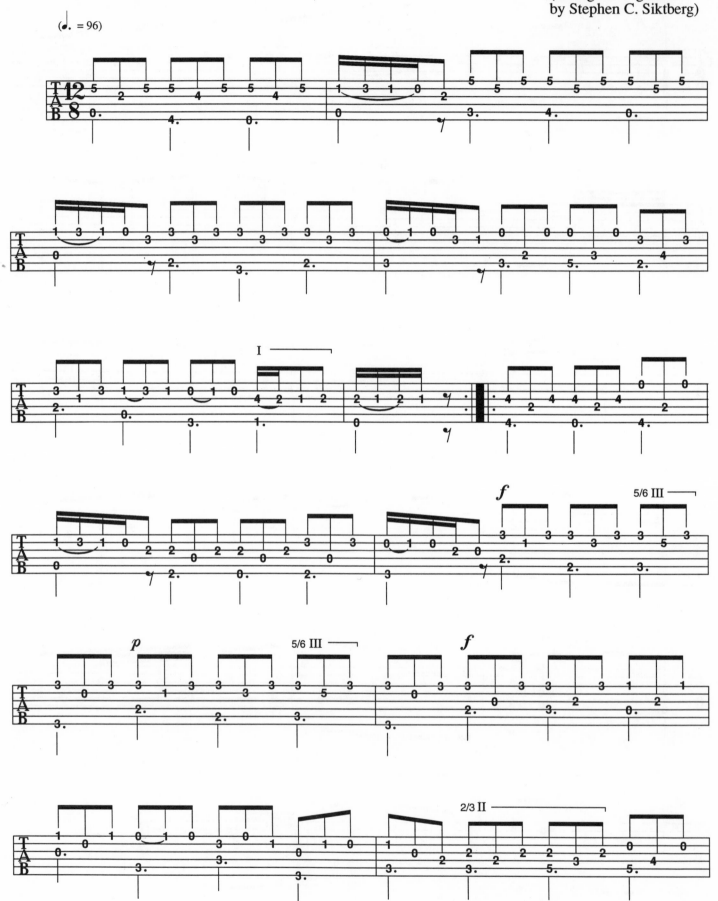

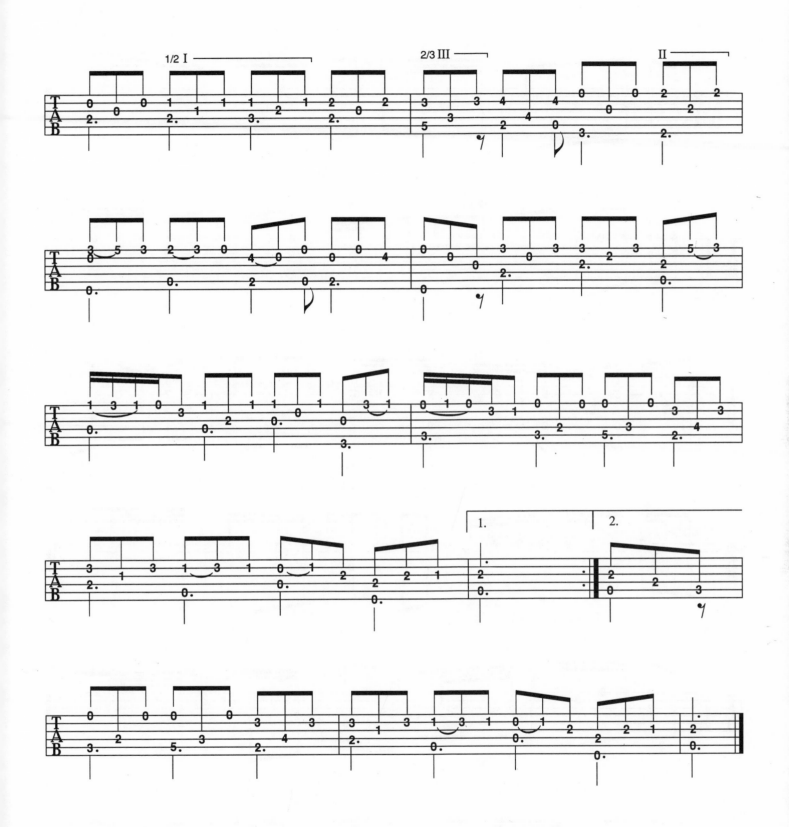

Les Tambourins

Francois Couperin
(arranged for guitar
by Stephen C. Siktberg)

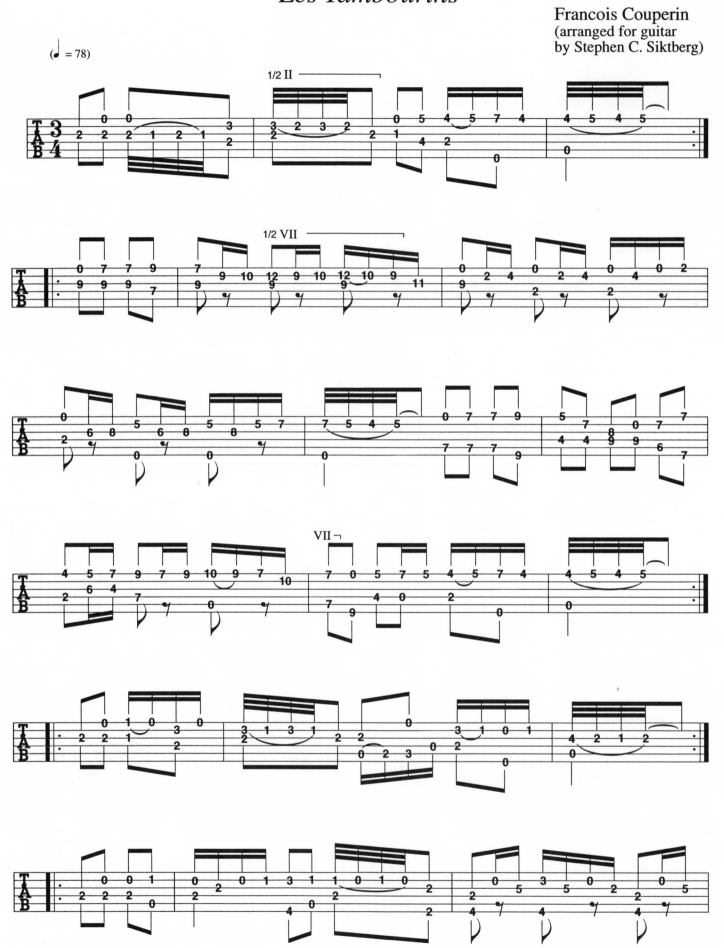

183

La Badine
(Rondeau)

Francois Couperin
(arranged for guitar
by Stephen C. Siktberg)

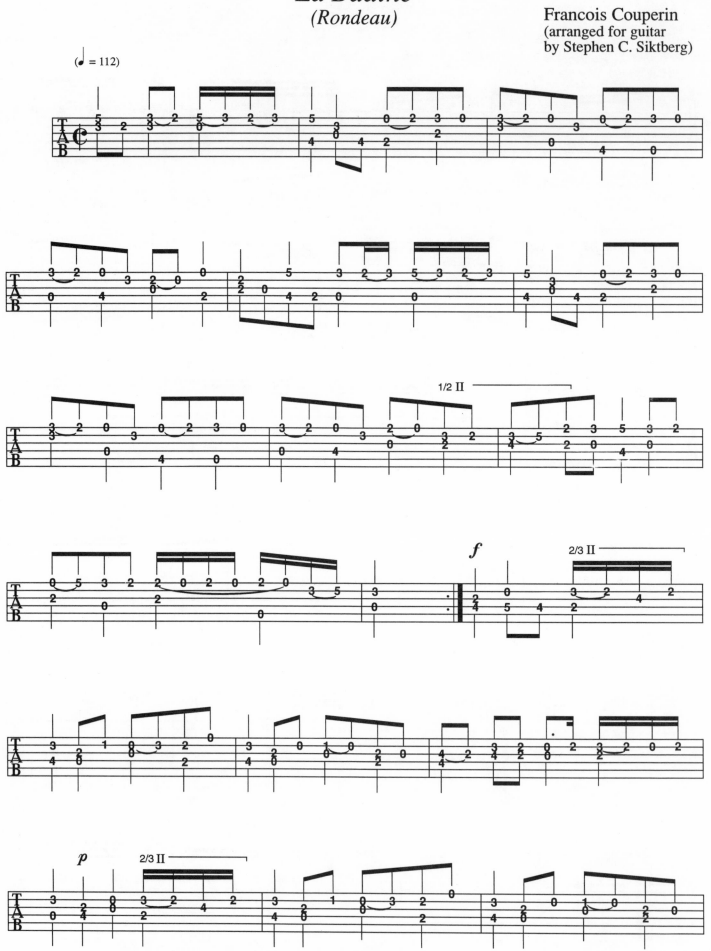

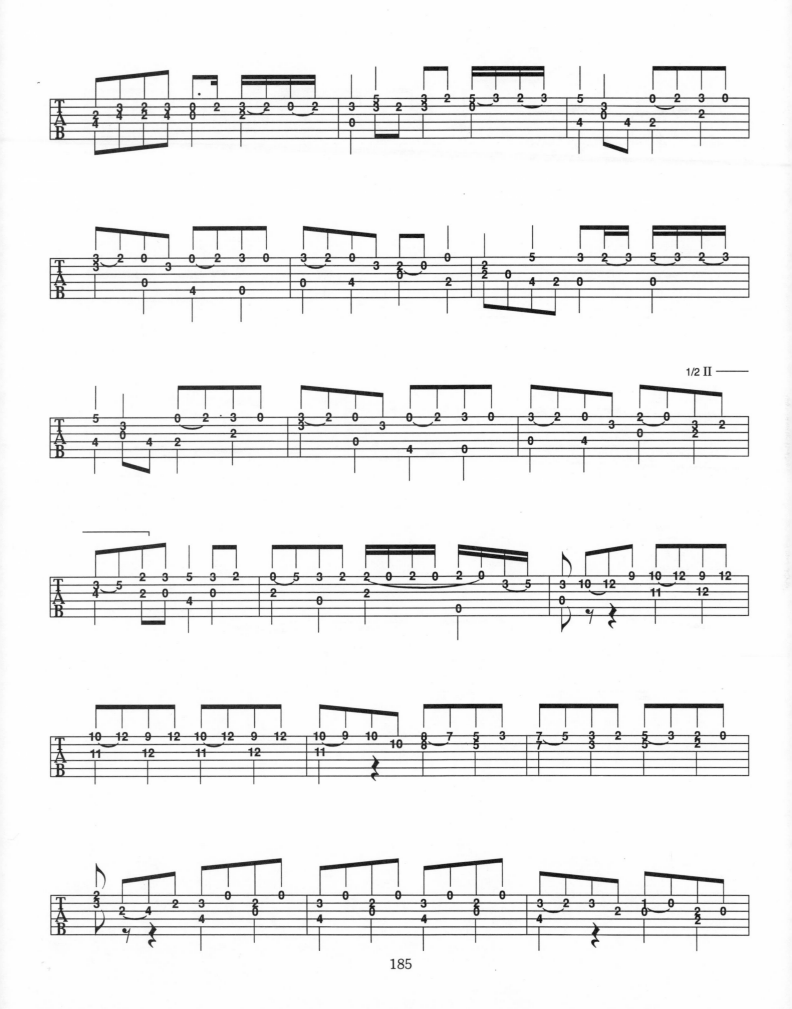

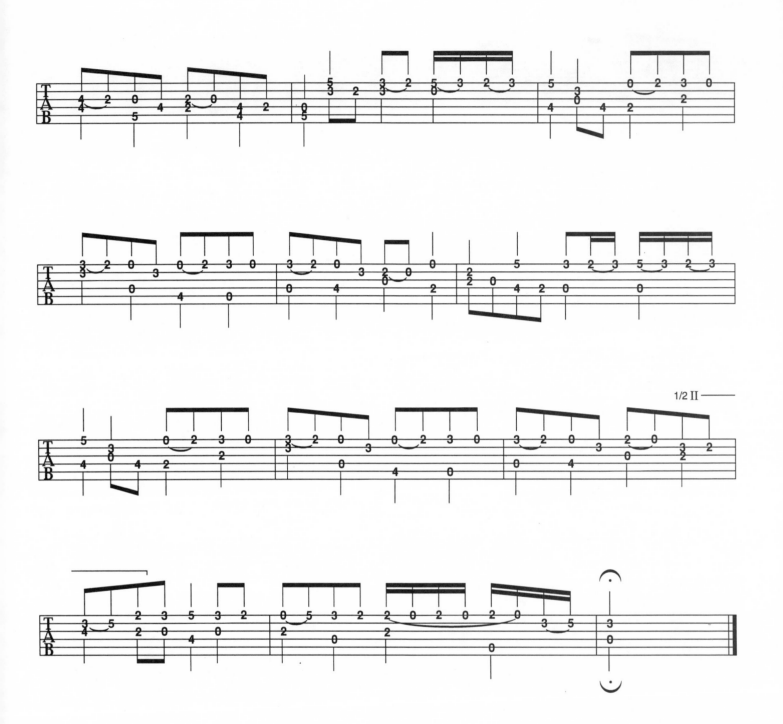

186

Les Bacchanales

Francois Couperin
(arranged for guitar
by Stephen C. Siktberg)

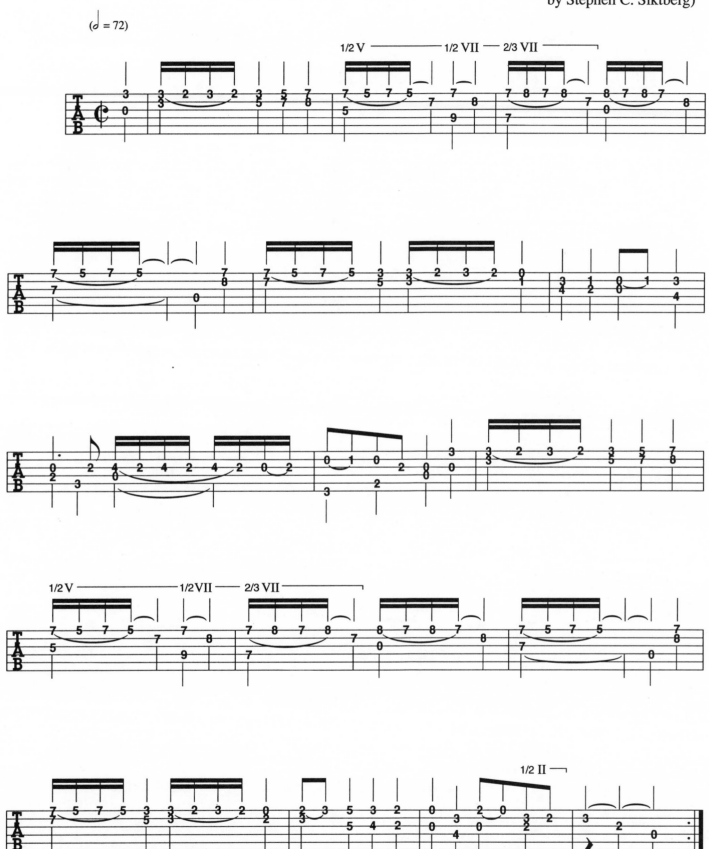

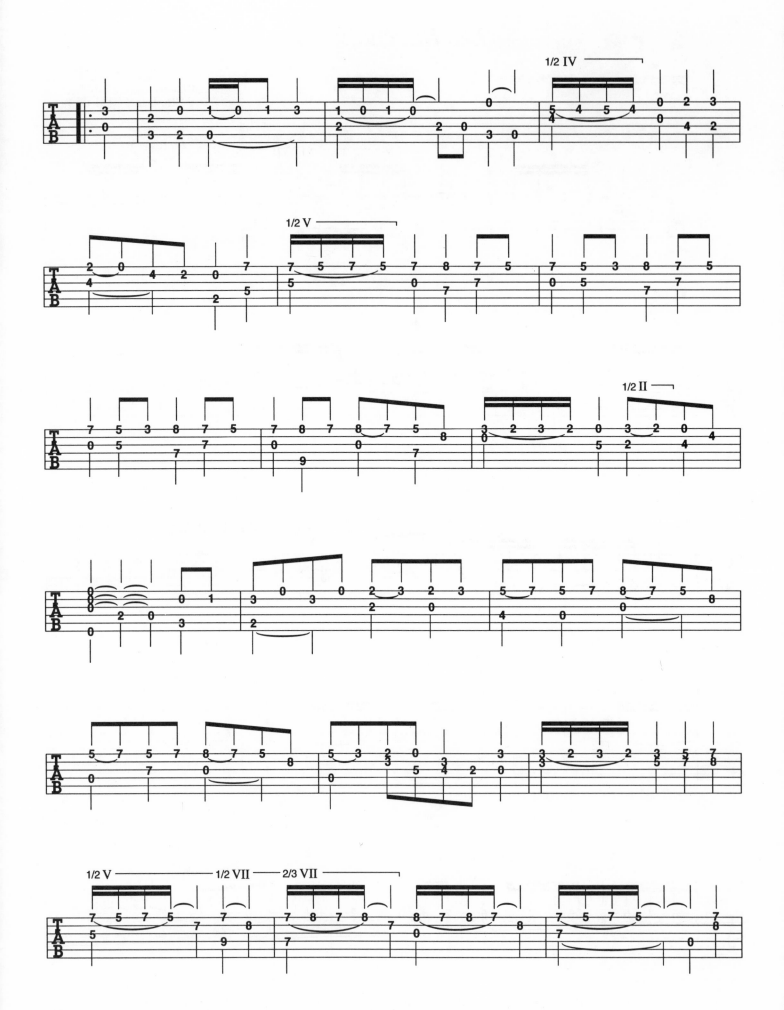

188

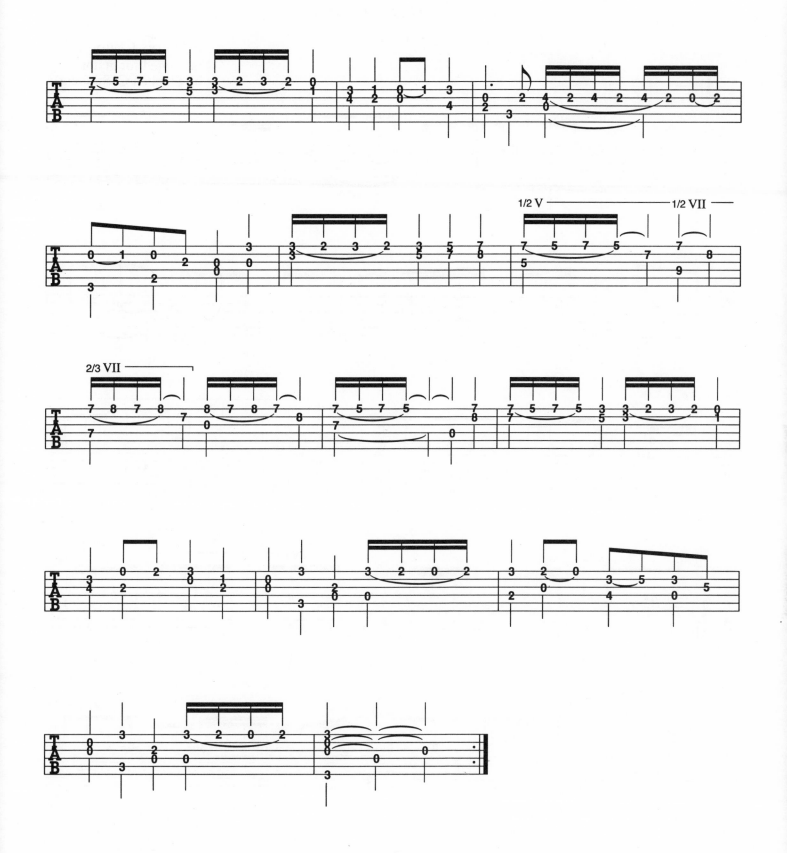

La Bourbonnoise
(Gavotte)

Francois Couperin
(arranged for guitar
by Stephen C. Siktberg)

Menuet en Rondeau

Jean-Philippe Rameau
arranged for guitar
by Stephen C. Siktberg)

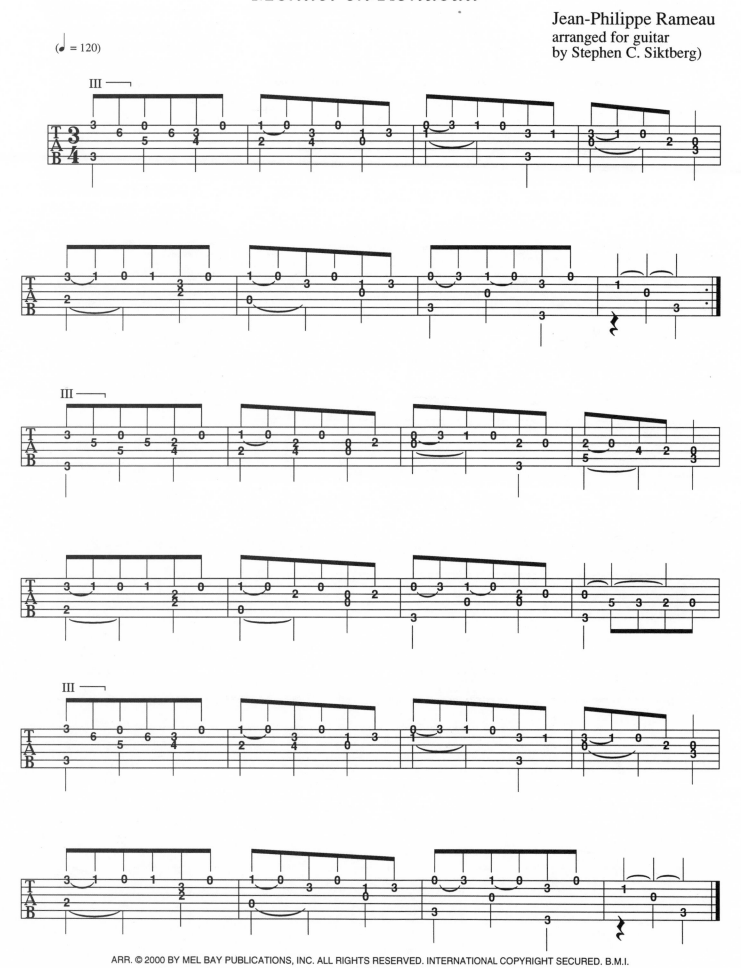

Menuet

Jean-Philippe Rameau
(arranged for guitar
by Stephen C. Siktberg)

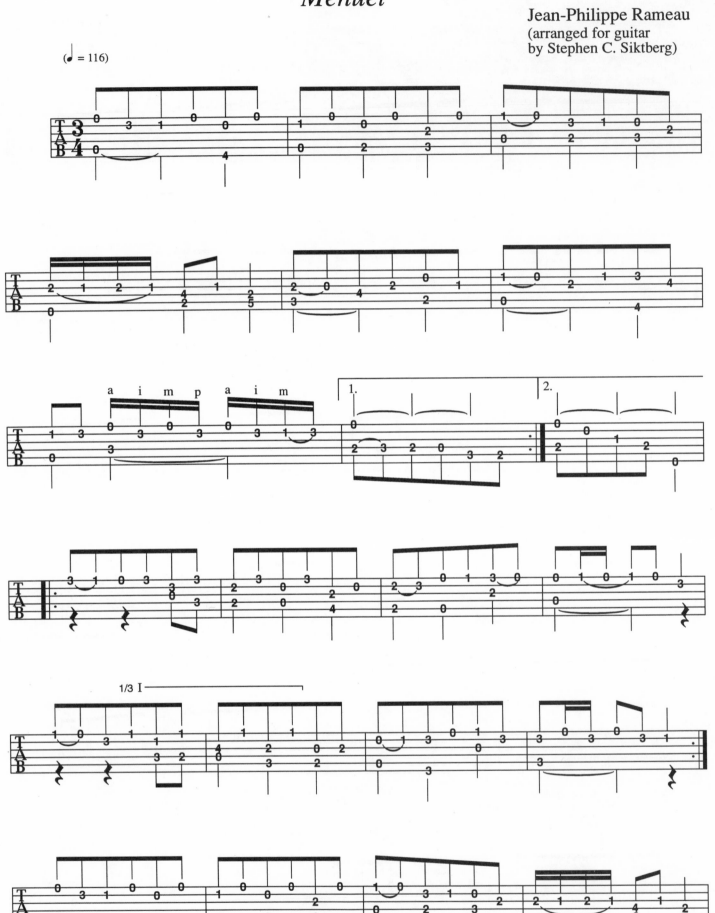

193

Sarabande 1

Jean-Philippe Rameau
(arranged for guitar
by Stephen C. Siktberg)

($\quad$ = 76)

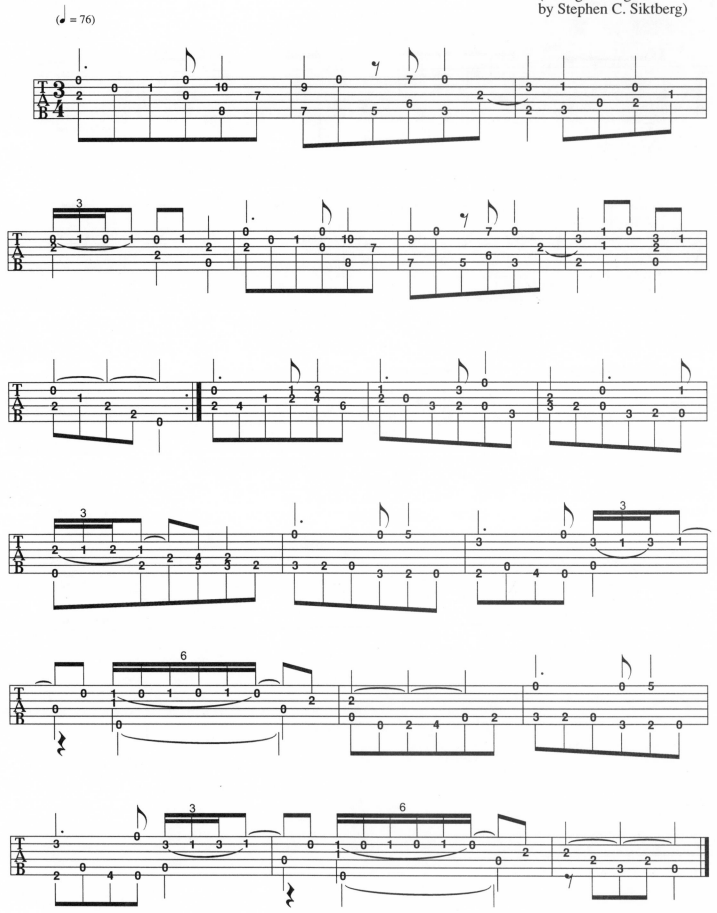

Sarabande 2

Jean-Philippe Rameau
(arranged for guitar
by Stephen C. Siktberg)

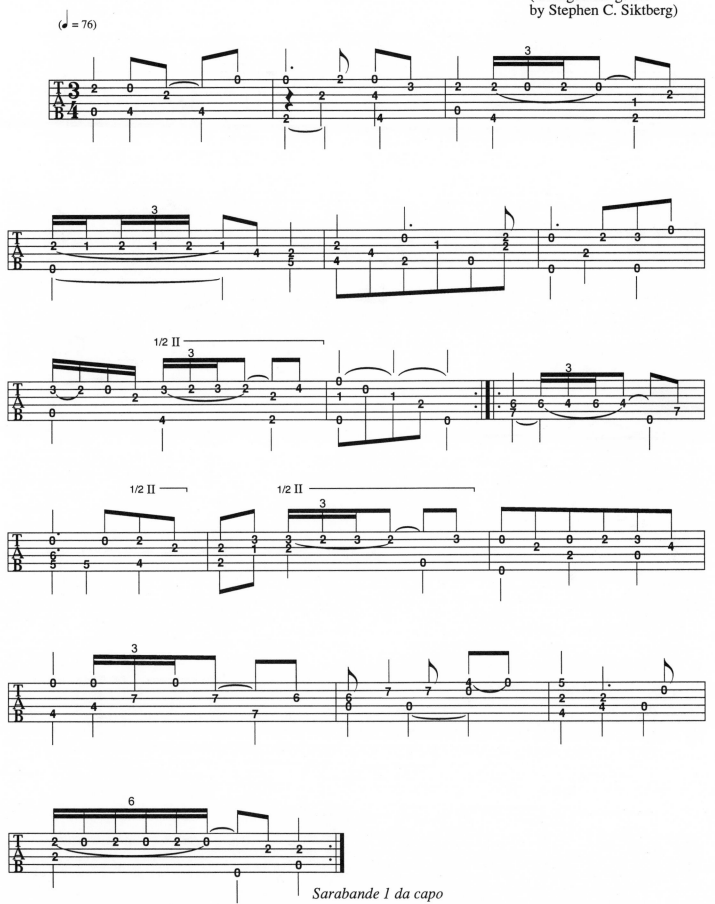

Sarabande 1 da capo

Gavotte en Rondeau

Jean-Philippe Rameau
(arranged for guitar
by Stephen C. Siktberg)

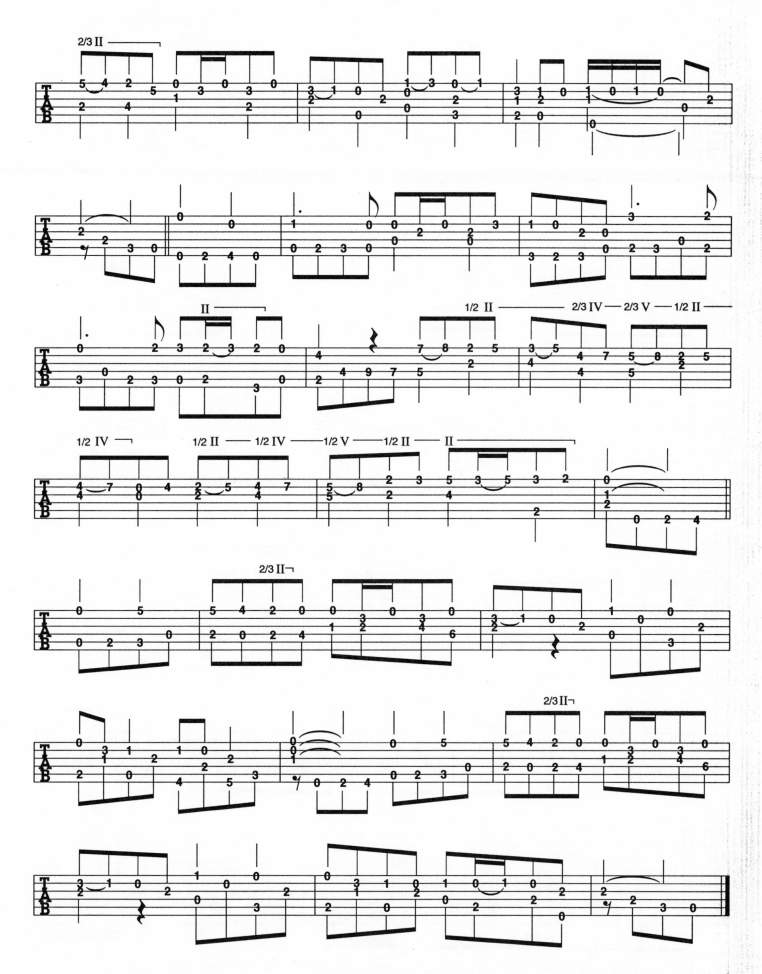

197

Les Tendres Plaintes
(Rondeau)

Jean-Philippe Rameau
(arranged for guitar
by Stephen C. Siktberg)

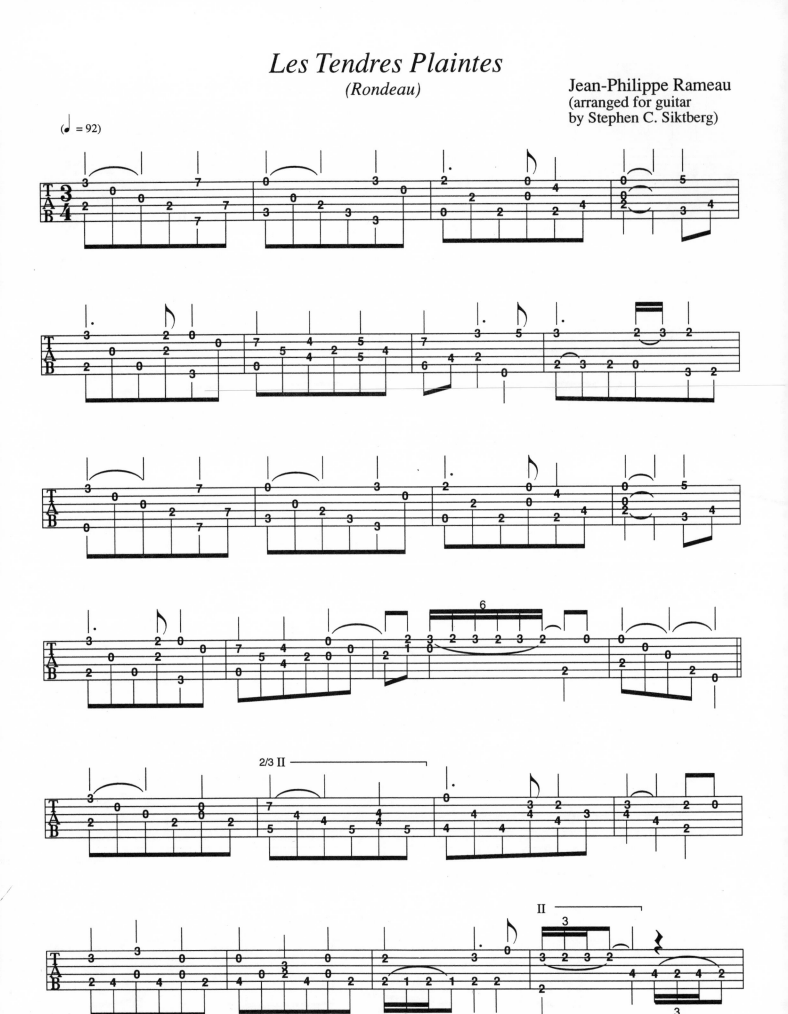

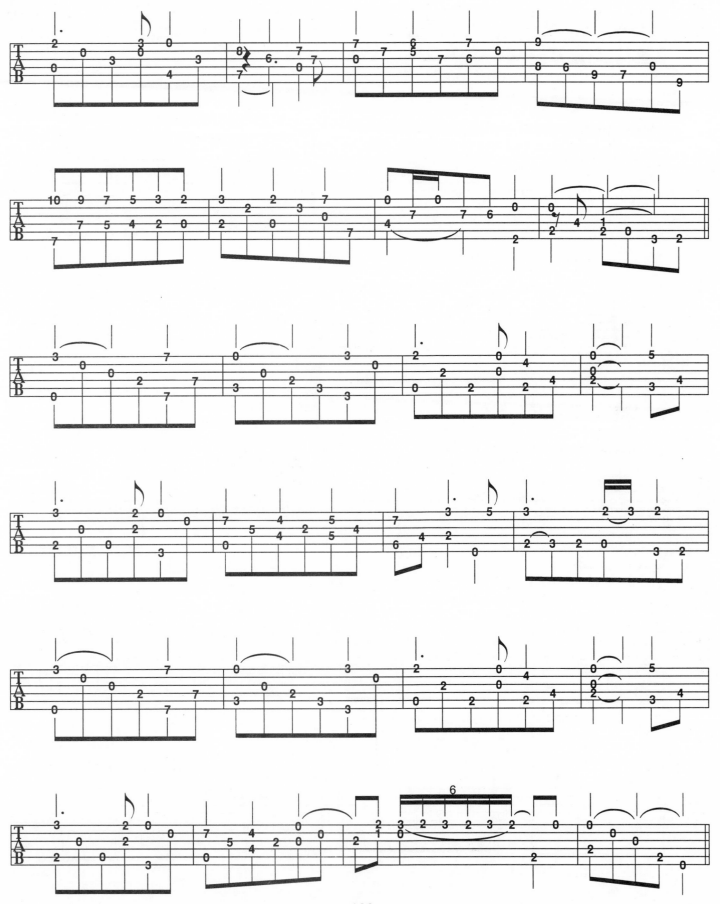

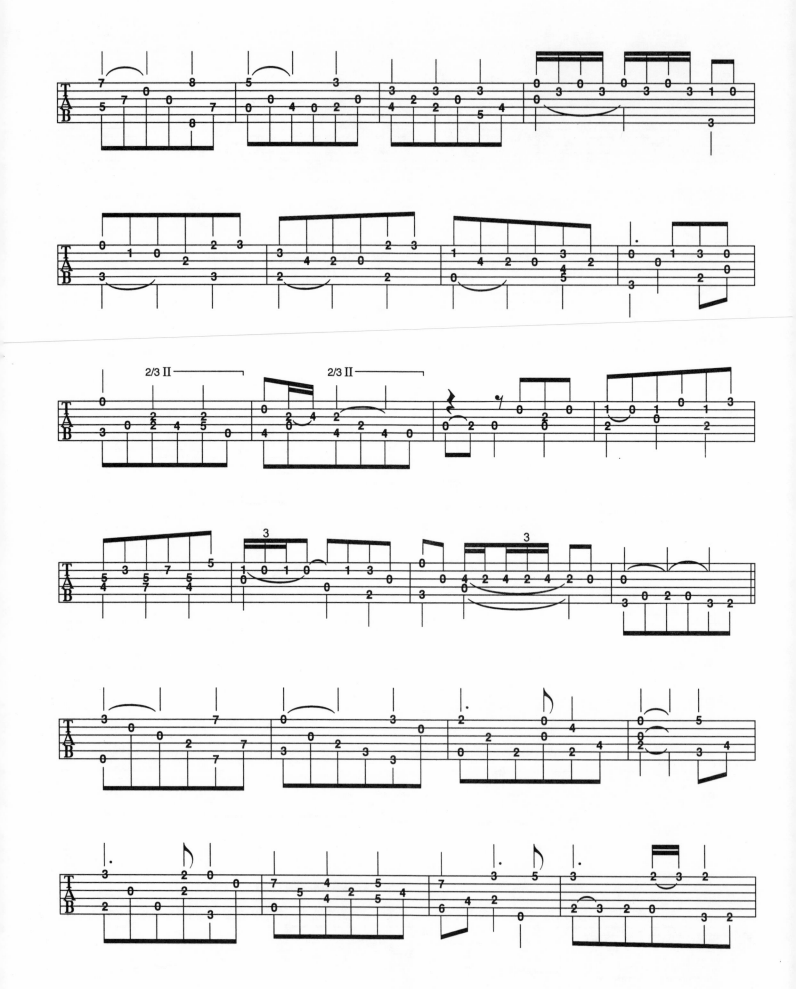

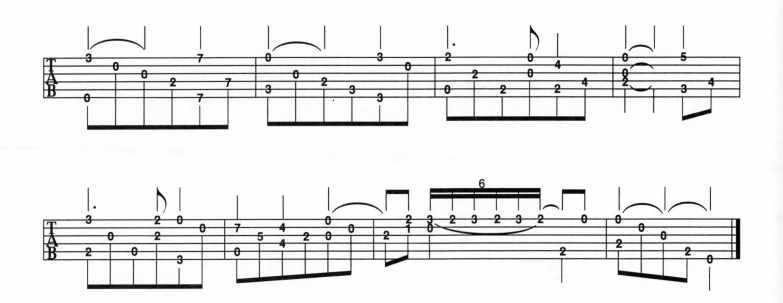

Menuet 1

Jean-Philippe Rameau
(arranged for guitar
by Stephen C. Siktberg)

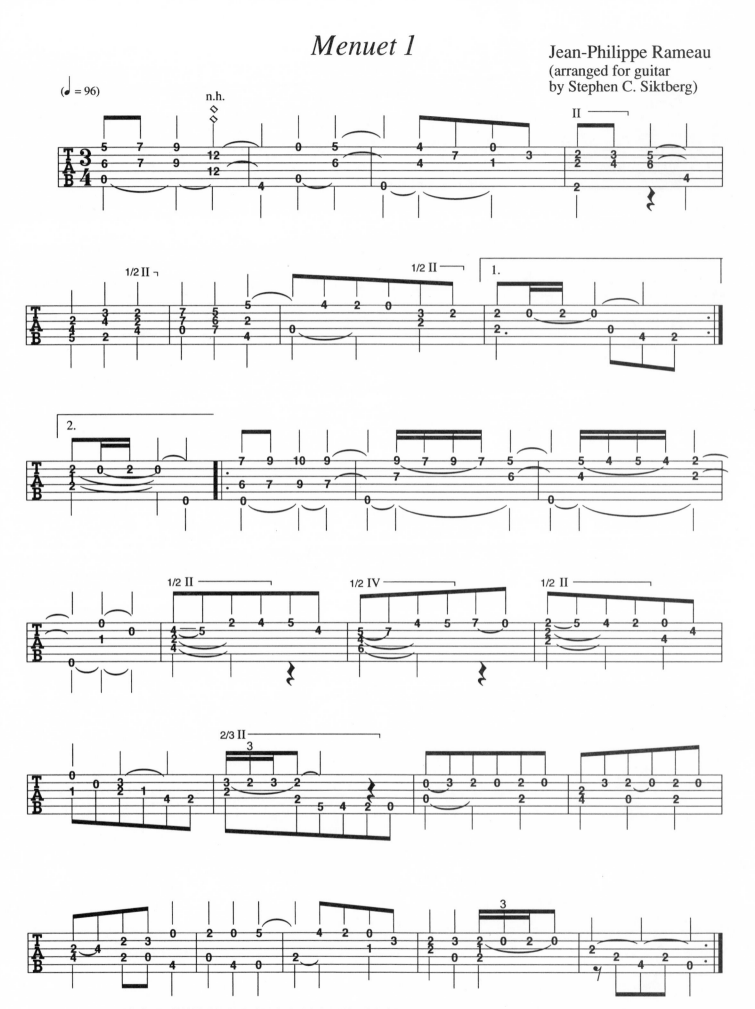

Menuet 2

Jean-Philippe Rameau
(arranged for guitar
by Stephen C. Siktberg)

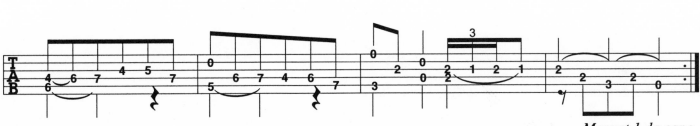

Menuet 1 da capo

Sonata in G
(K431)

Domenico Scarlatti
(arranged for guitar
by Stephen C. Siktberg)

6th = D

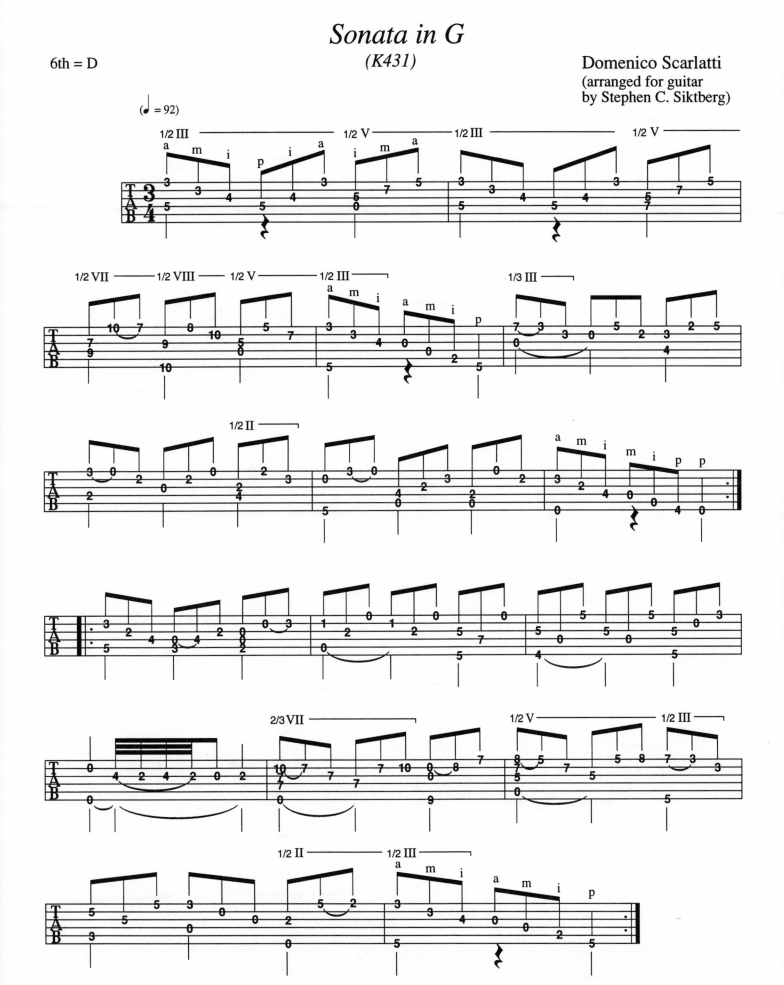

Sonata in Dm
(K434)

Domenico Scarlatti
(arranged for guitar
by Stephen C. Siktberg)

Andante
(♪ = 76)

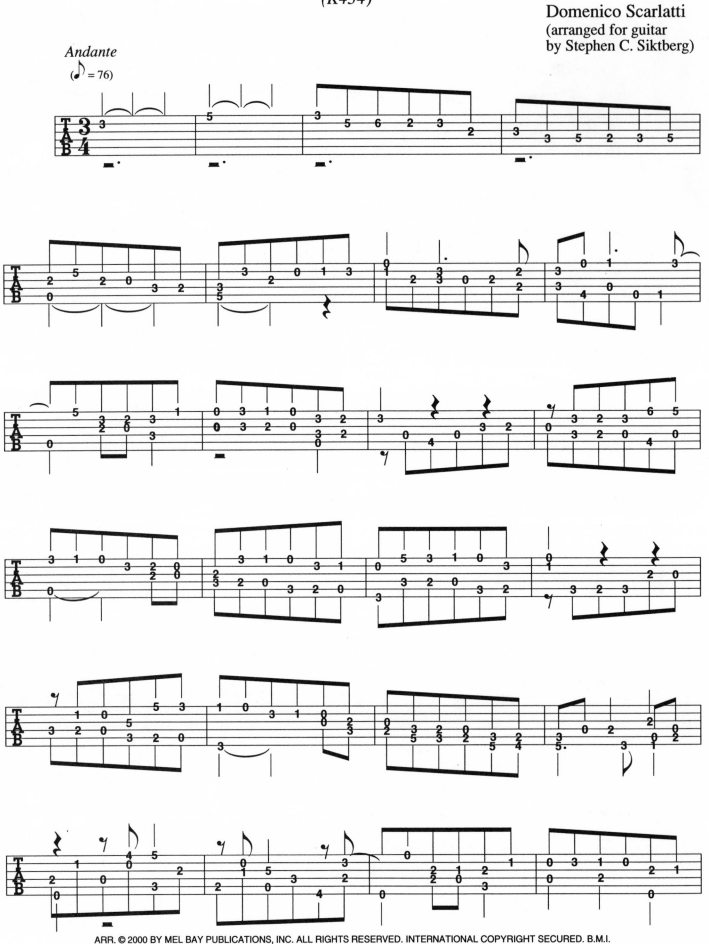

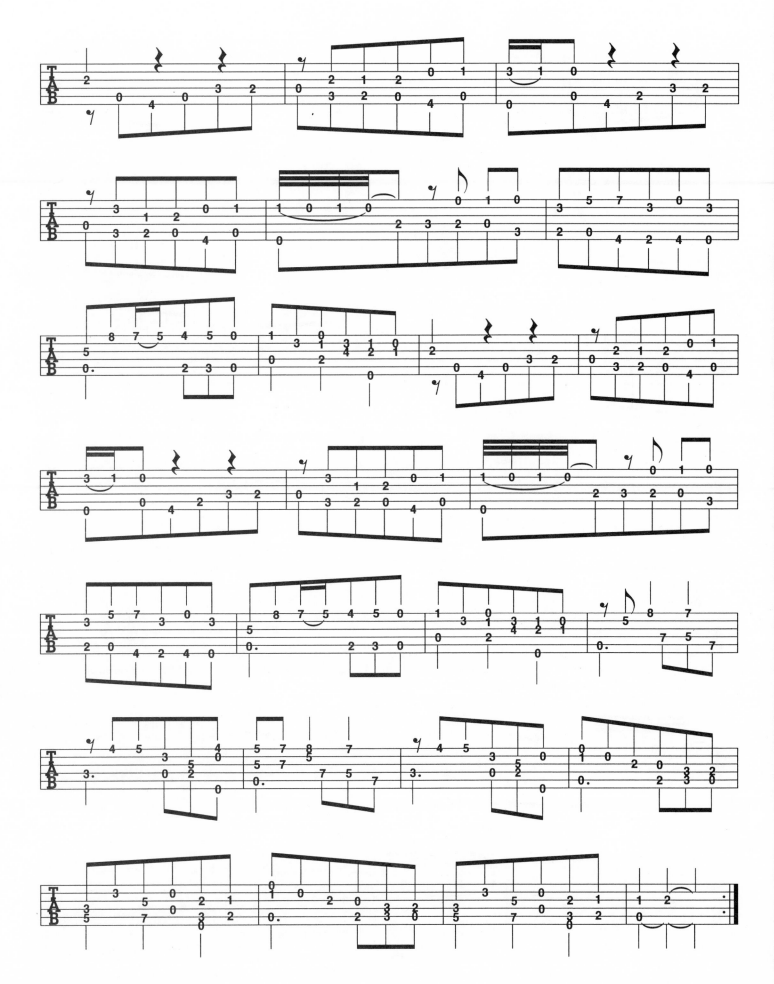

207

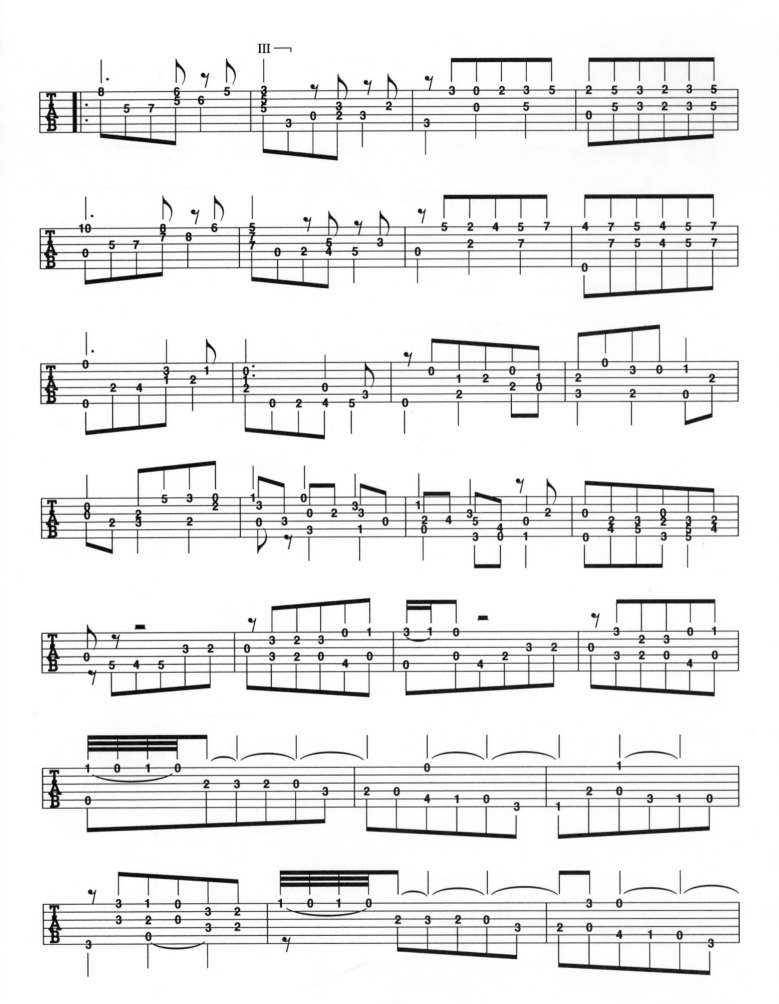

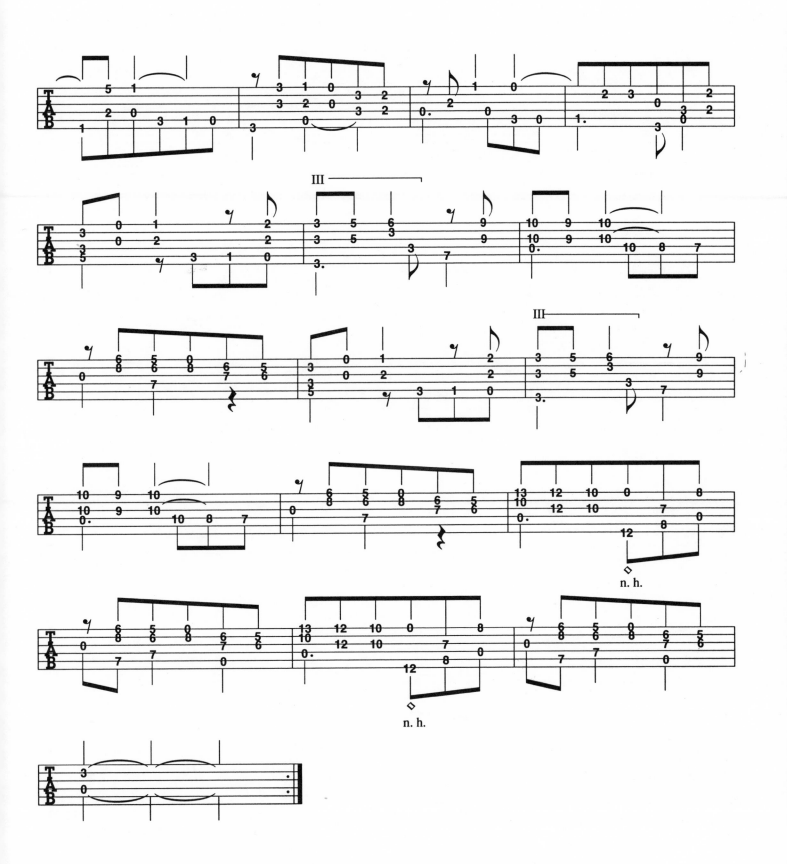

209

Sonata in D
(K414)

Domenico Scarlatti
(arranged for guitar
by Stephen C. Siktberg)

6th = D

(♩ = 120)

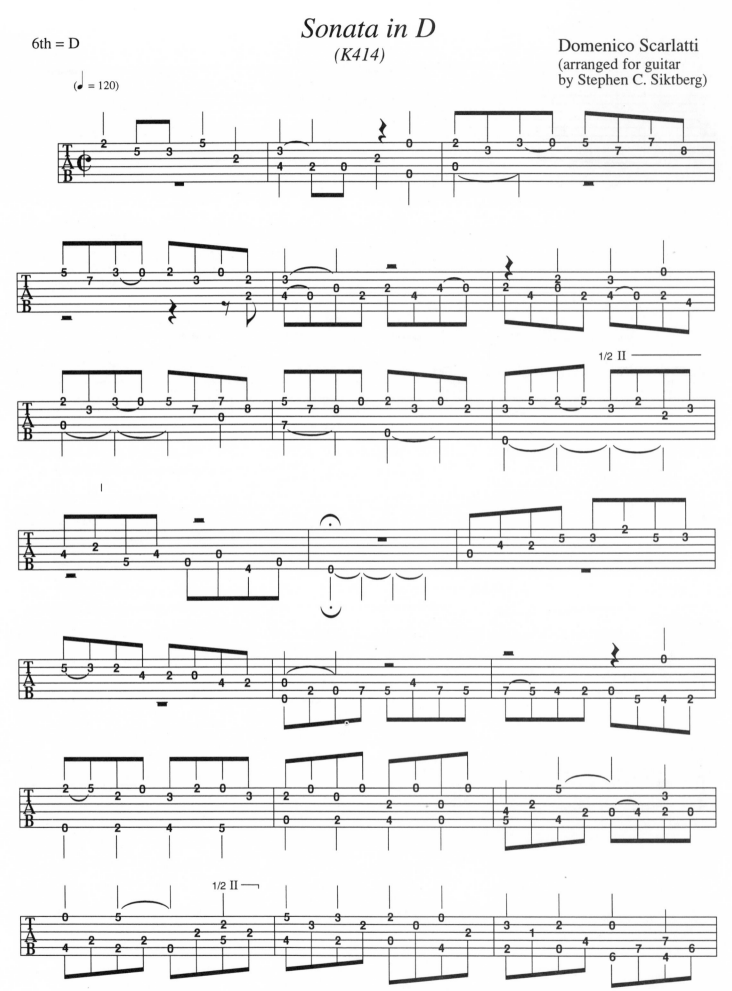

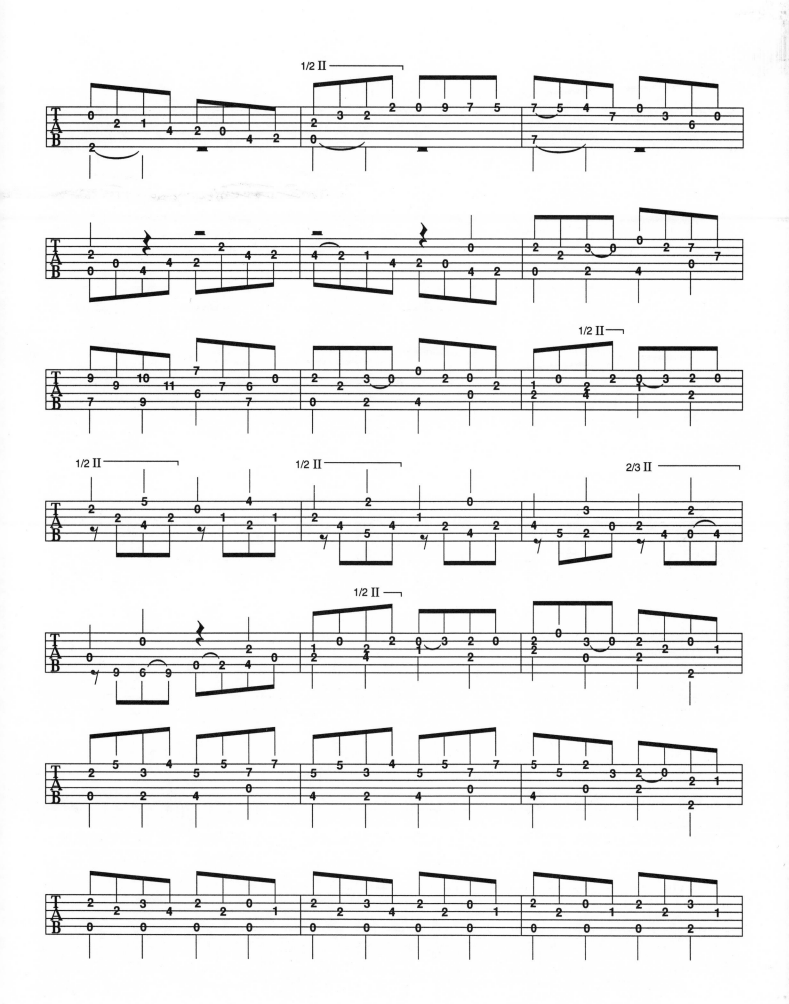

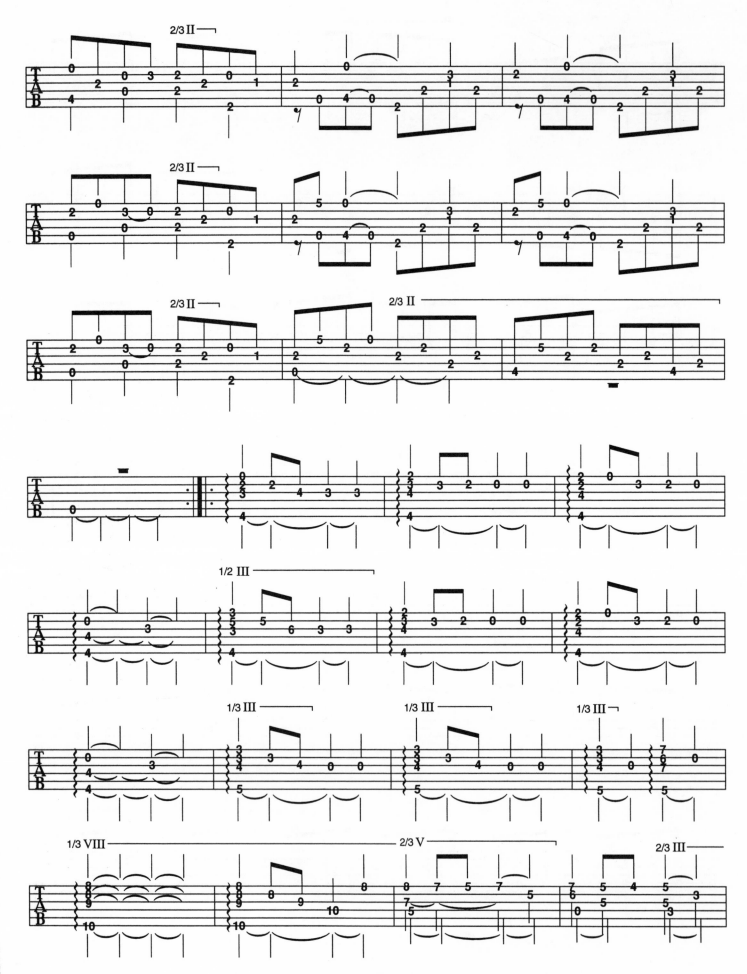

212

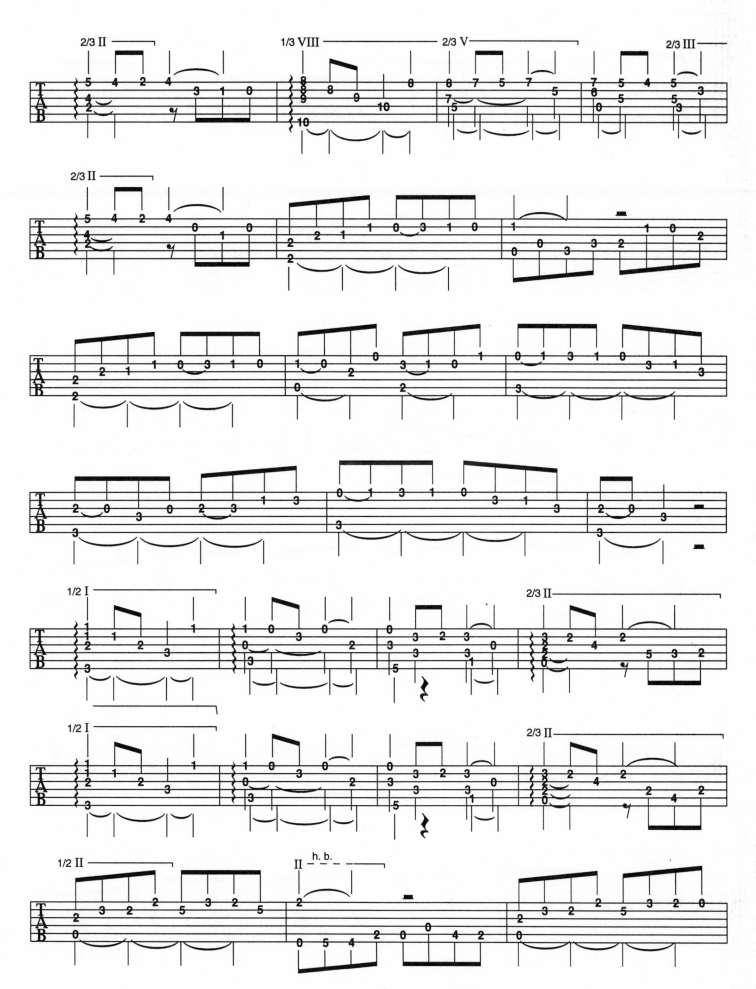

213

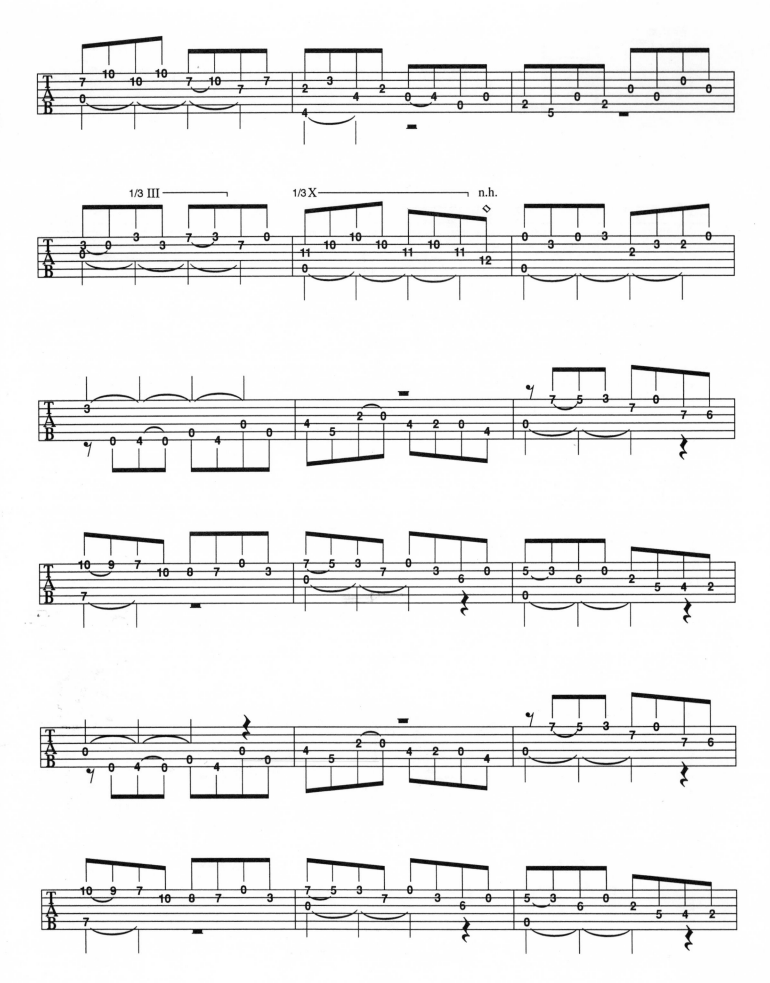

214

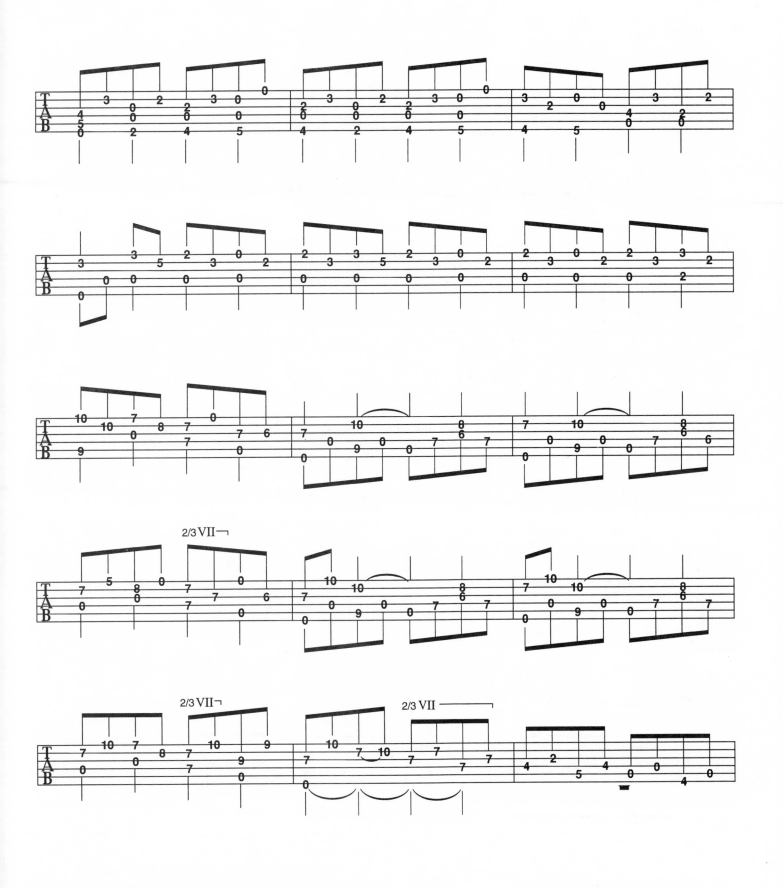

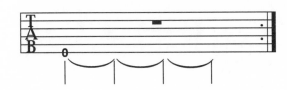

Sonata in A
(K428)

Domenico Scarlatti
(arranged for guitar
by Stephen C. Siktberg)

3rd = F#

(♩ = 104)

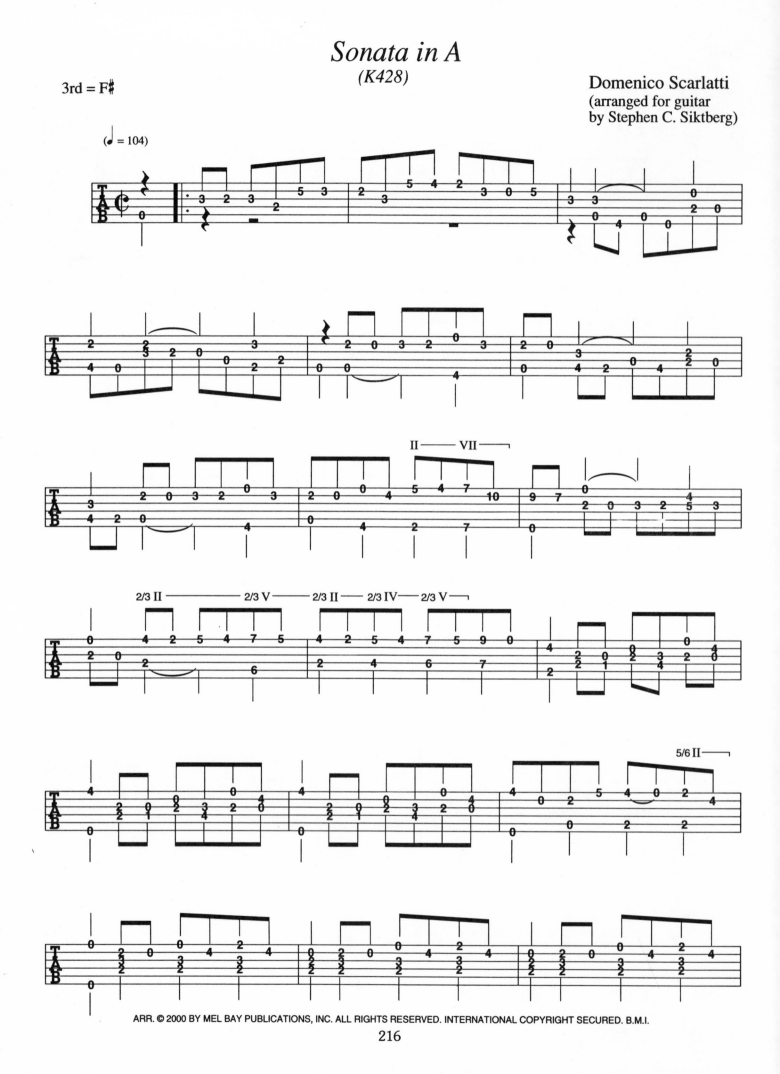

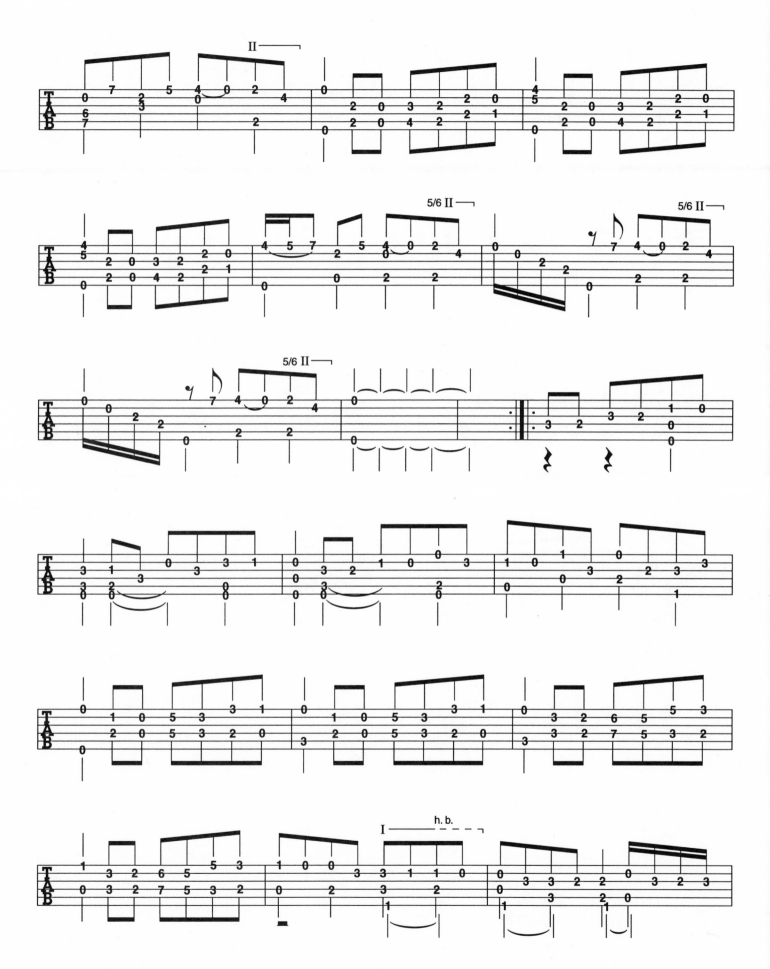

217

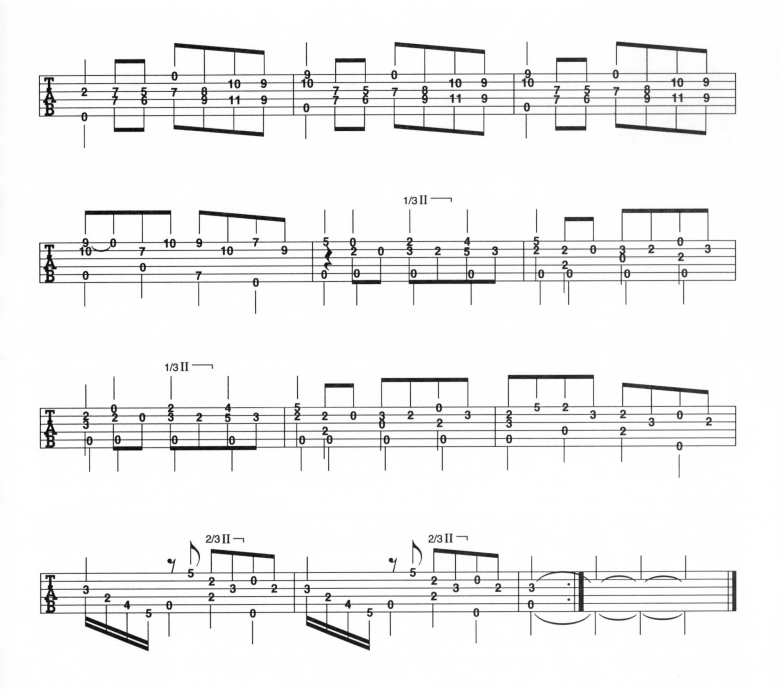

Fantasia in Em

George Philip Telemann
(arranged for guitar
by Stephen C. Siktberg)

Tempo di Minuetto
(♪ = 100)

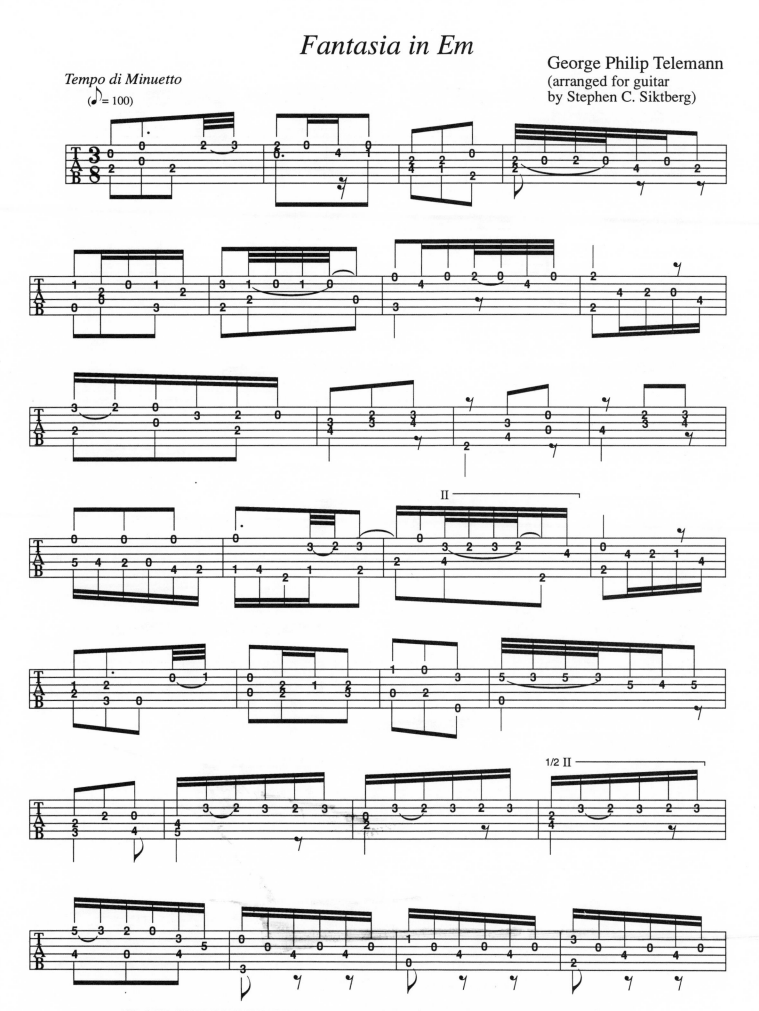

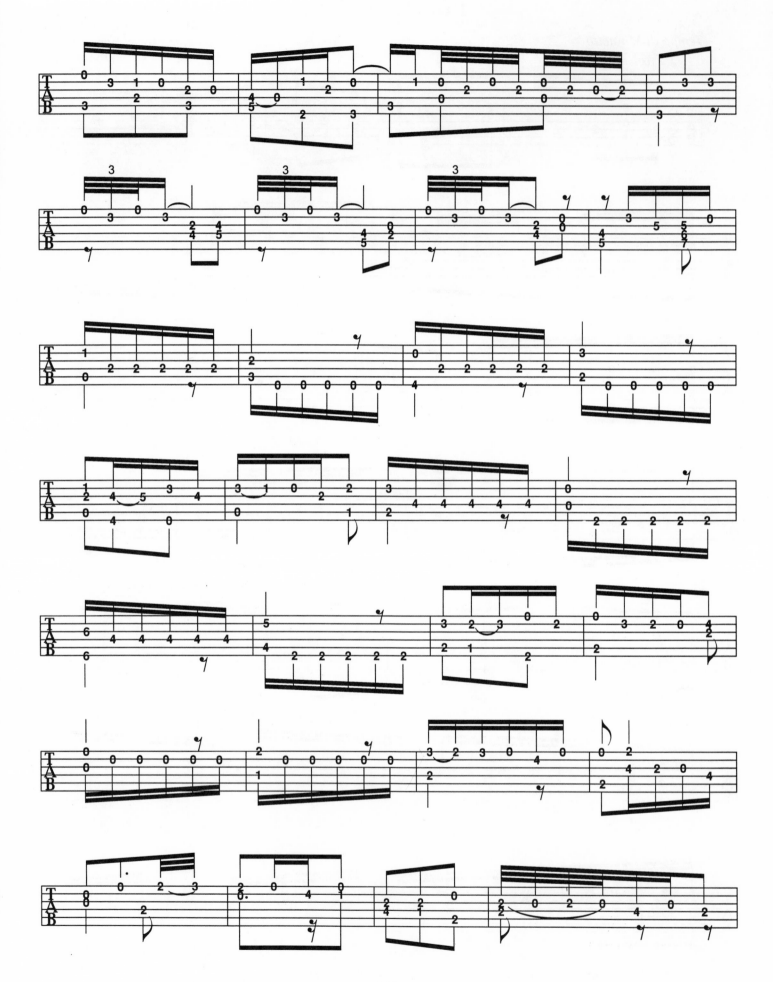

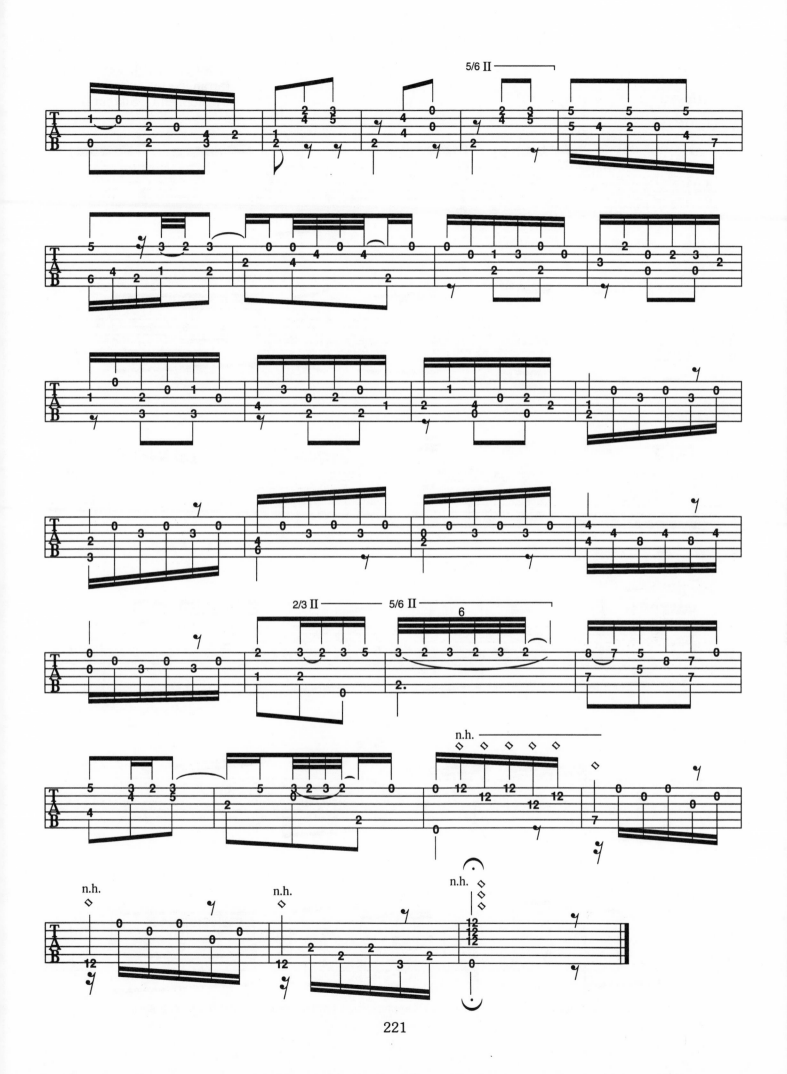

221

Fantasia in D

George Philip Telemann
(arranged for guitar
by Stephen C. Siktberg)

Allegro
(♪ = 160)

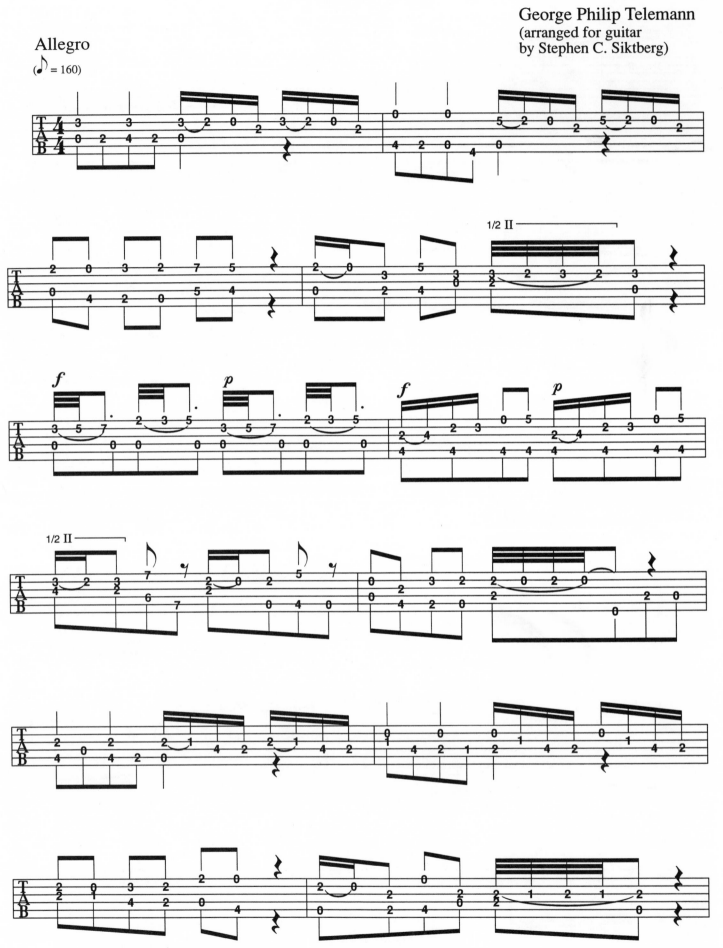

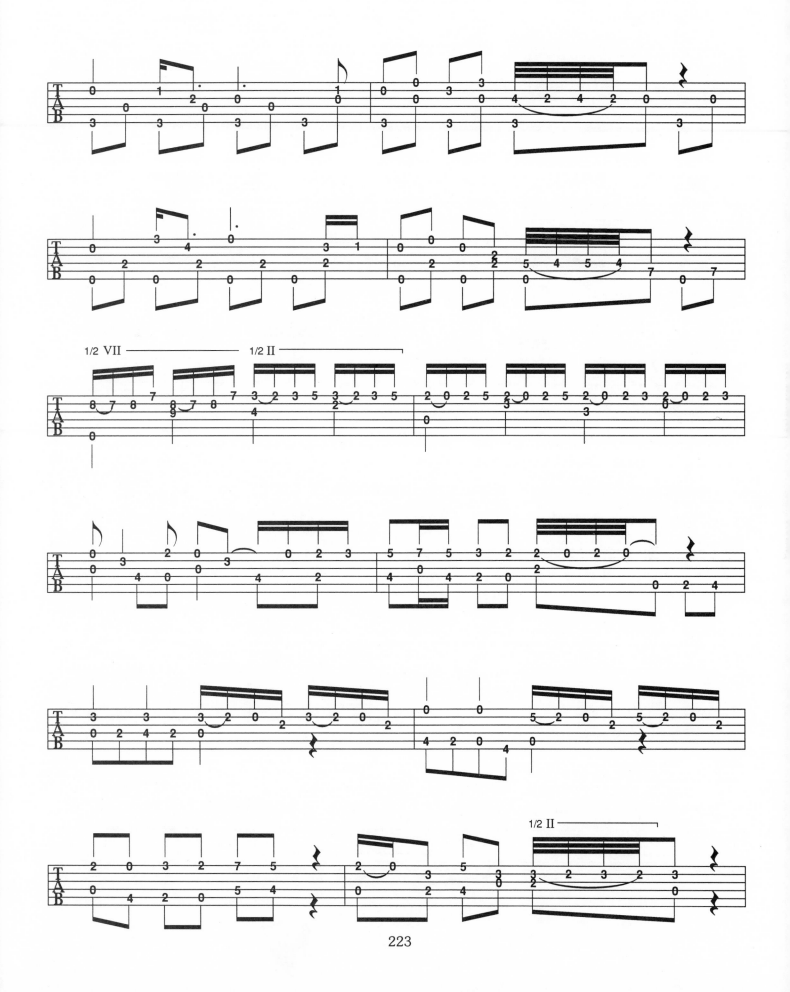

223

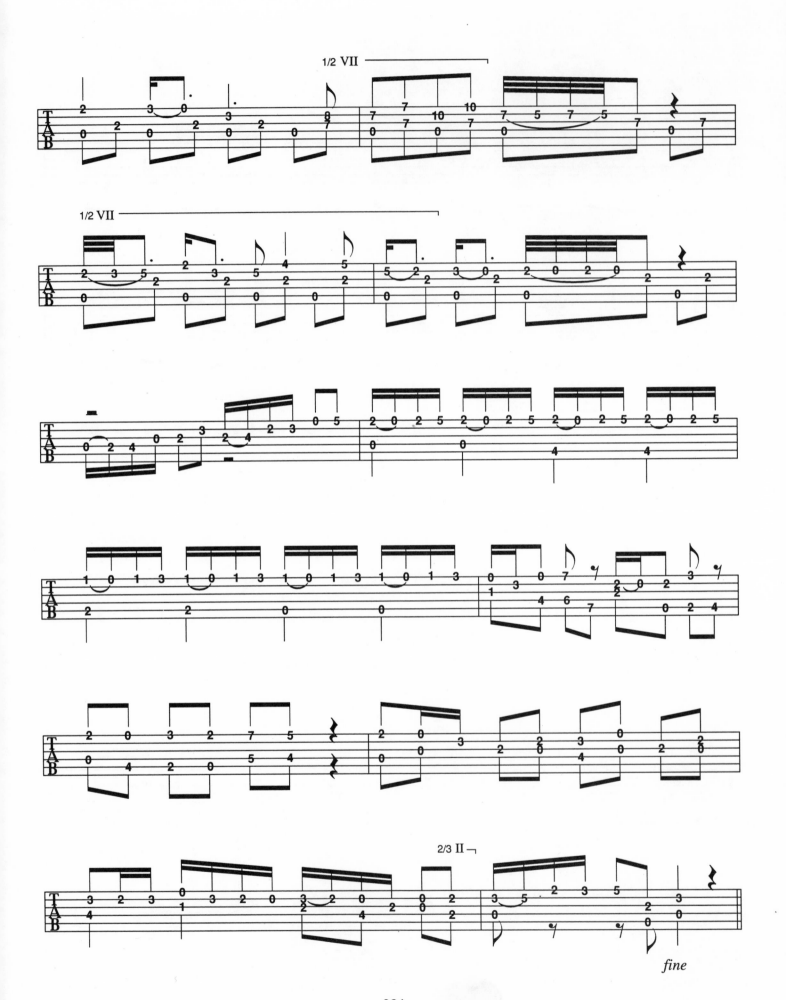

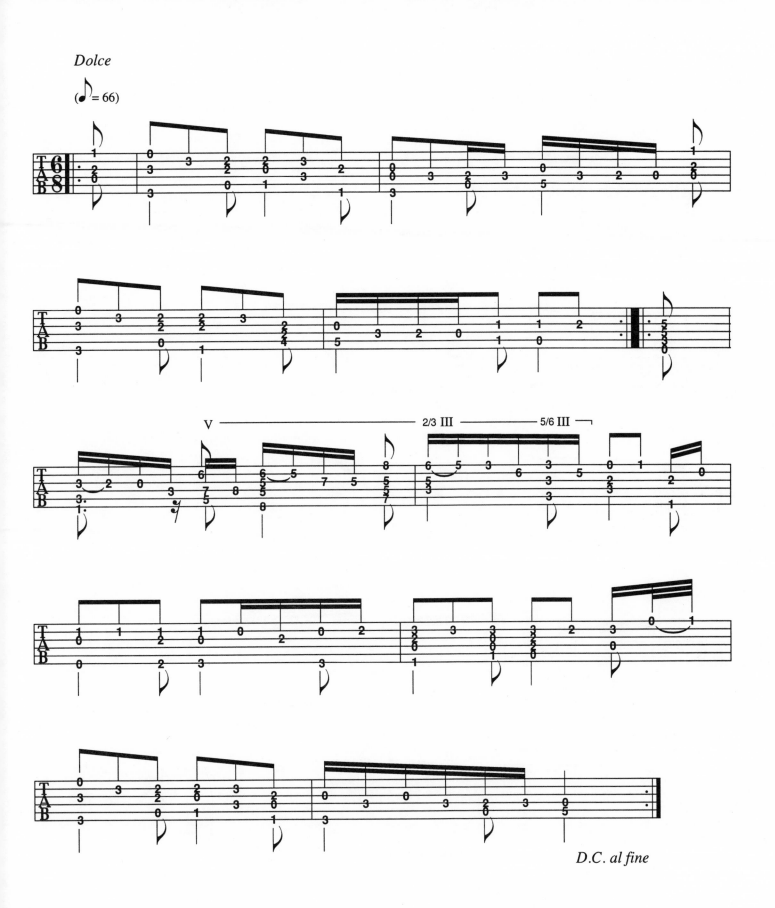

Dolce

D.C. al fine

225

Fantasia in D

George Philip Telemann
(arranged for guitar
by Stephen C. Siktberg)

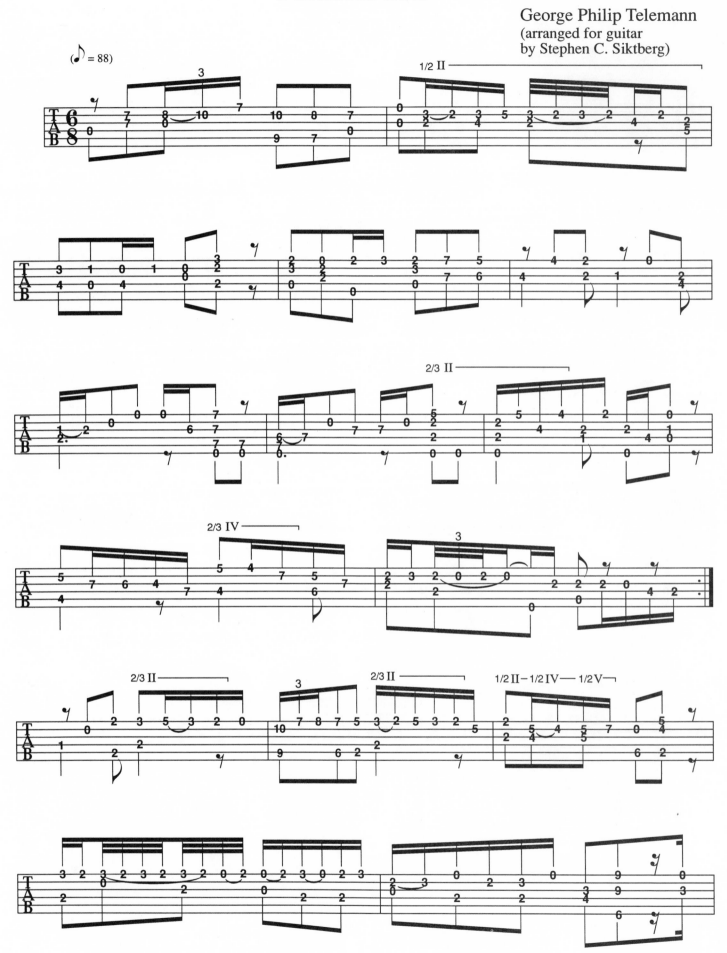

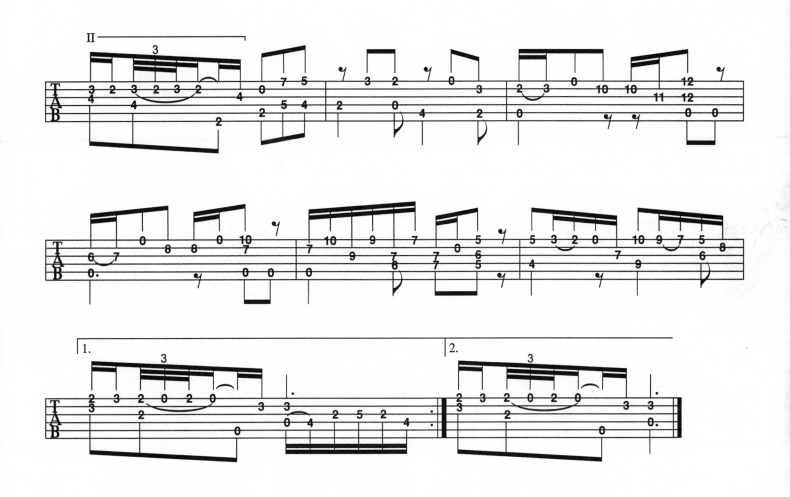

Fantasia in Dm

George Philip Telemann
(arranged for guitar
by Stephen C. Siktberg)

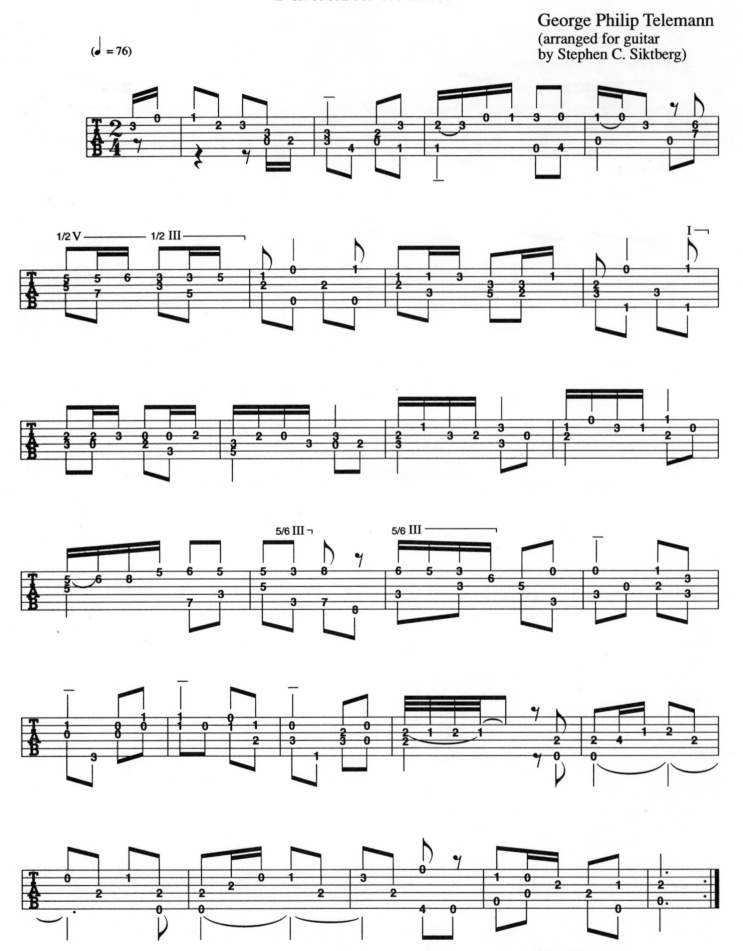

Fantasia in Am

George Philip Telemann
(arranged for guitar
by Stephen C. Siktberg)

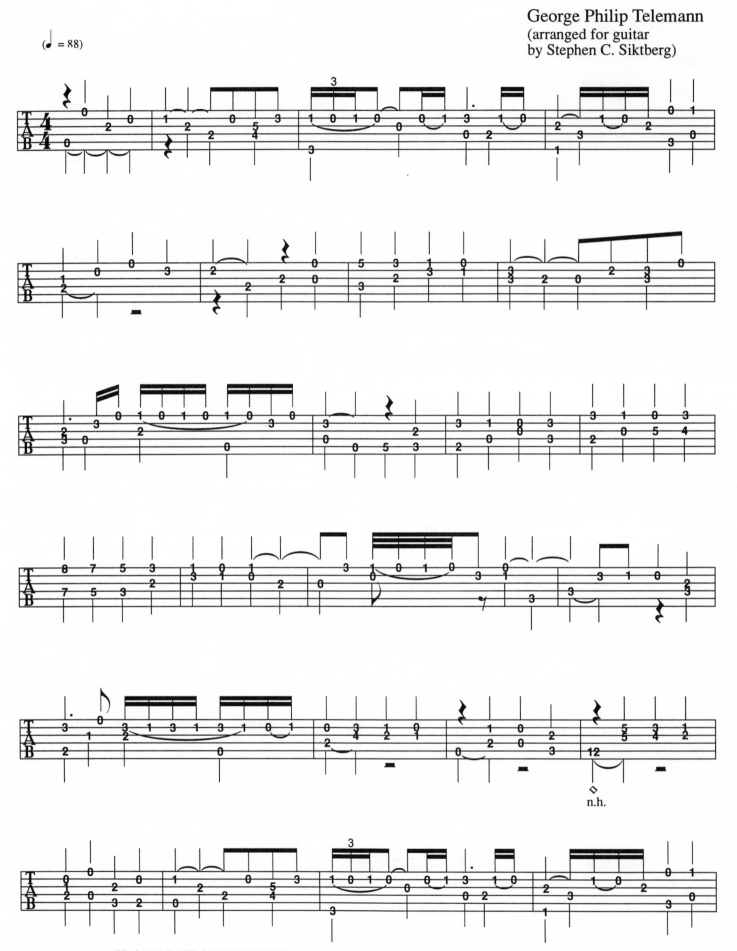

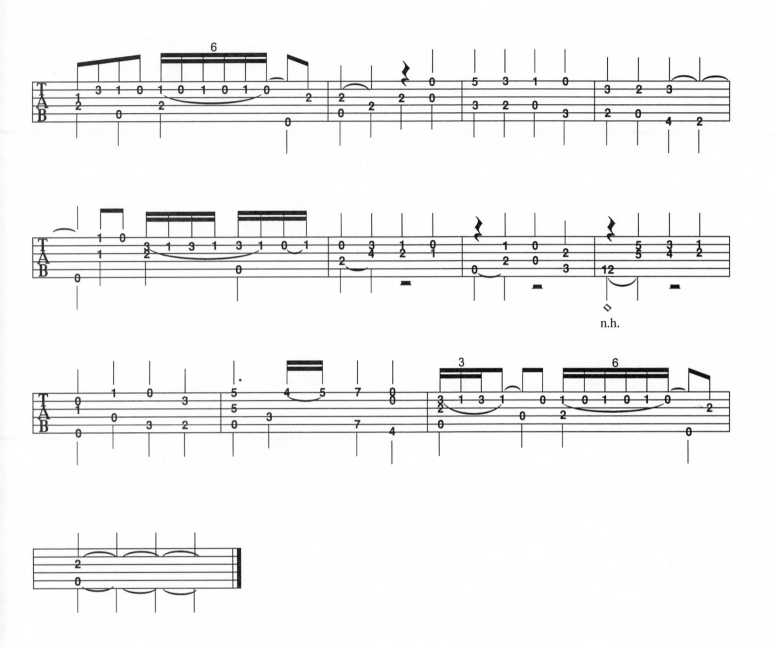

Fantasia in C

George Philip Telemann
(arranged for guitar
by Stephen C. Siktberg)

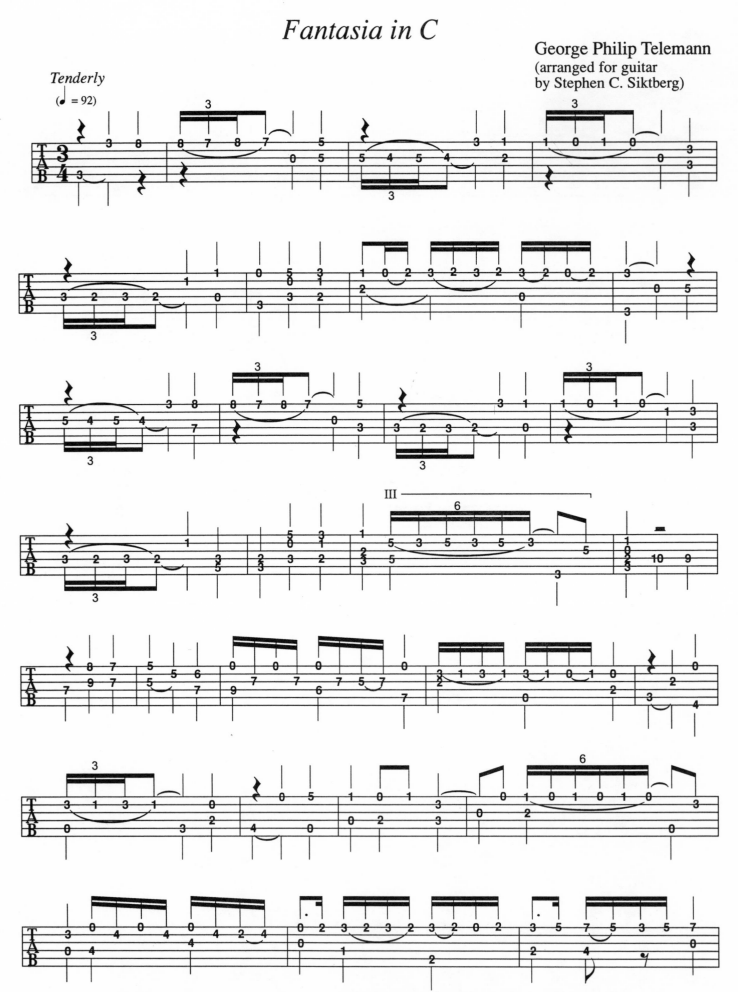

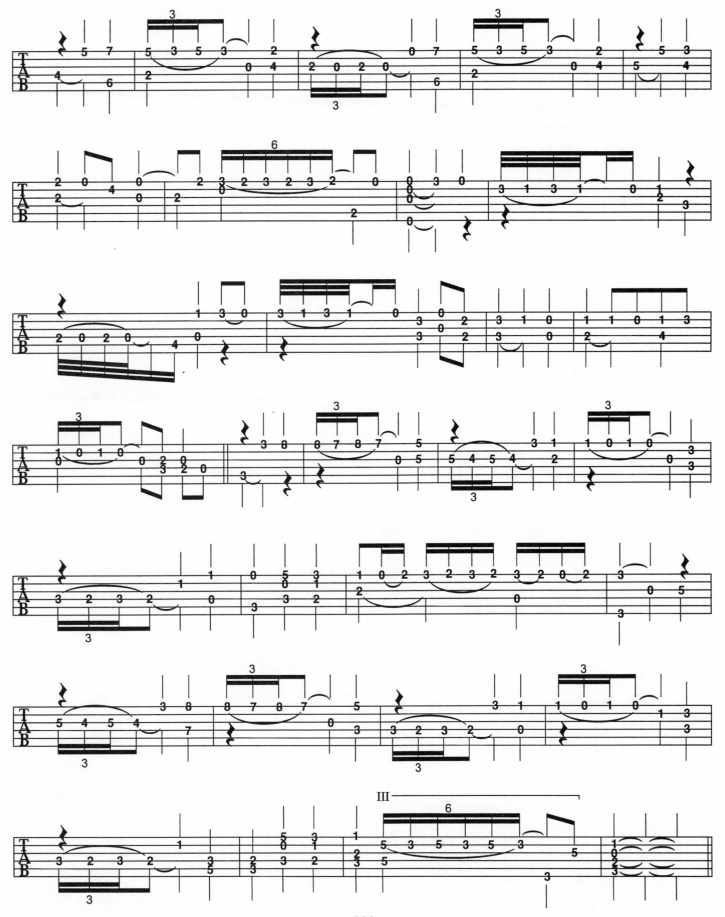

Gaily

($\flat$ = 164)

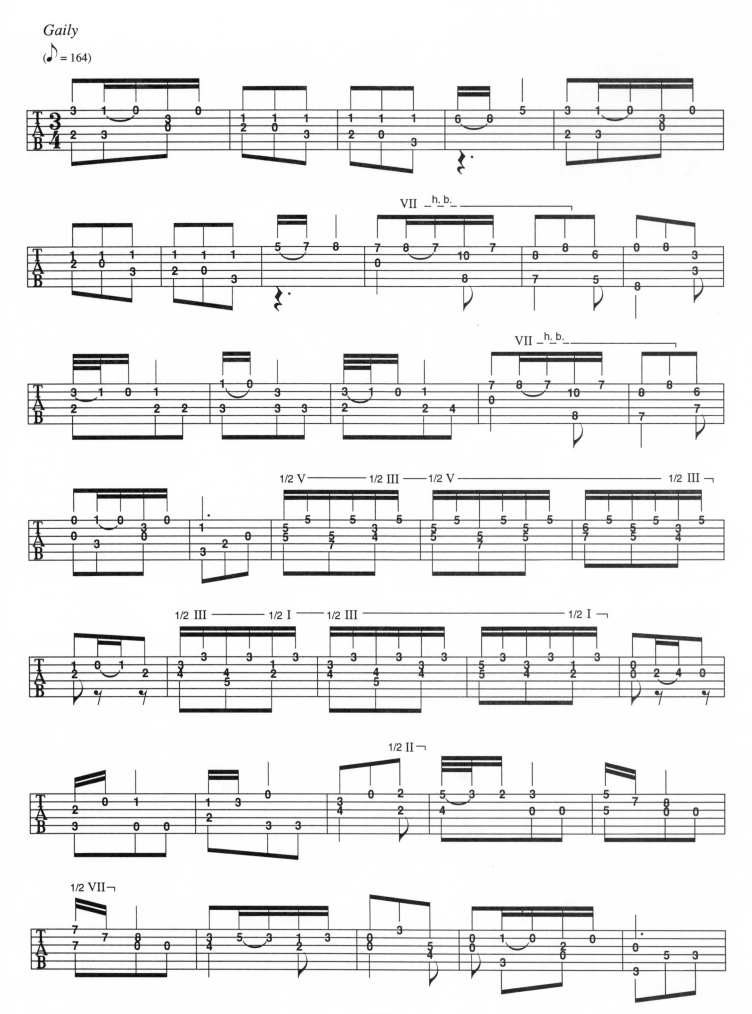

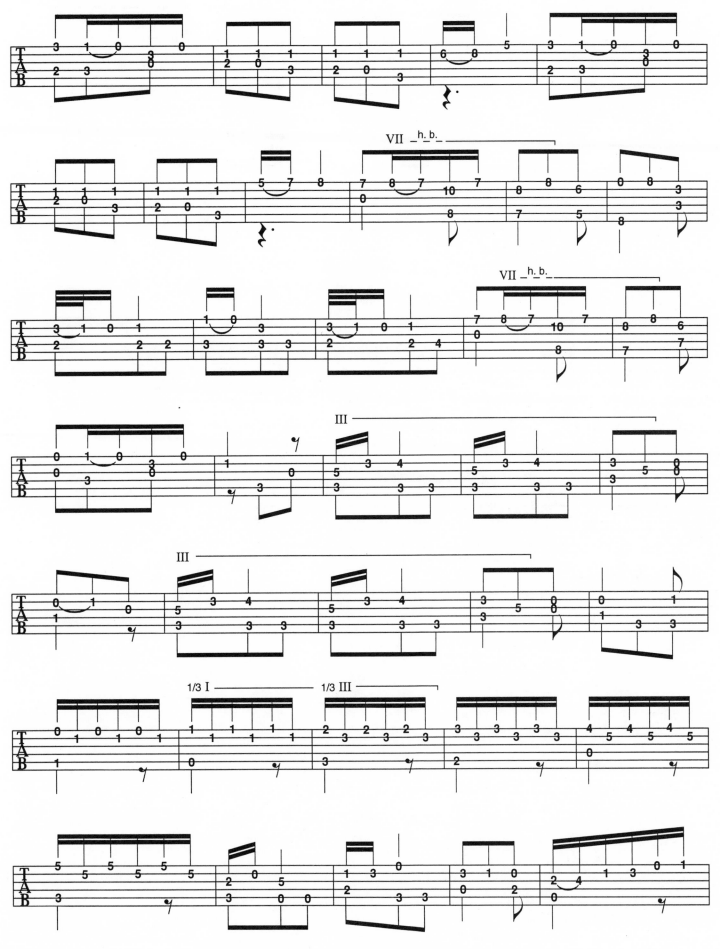

235

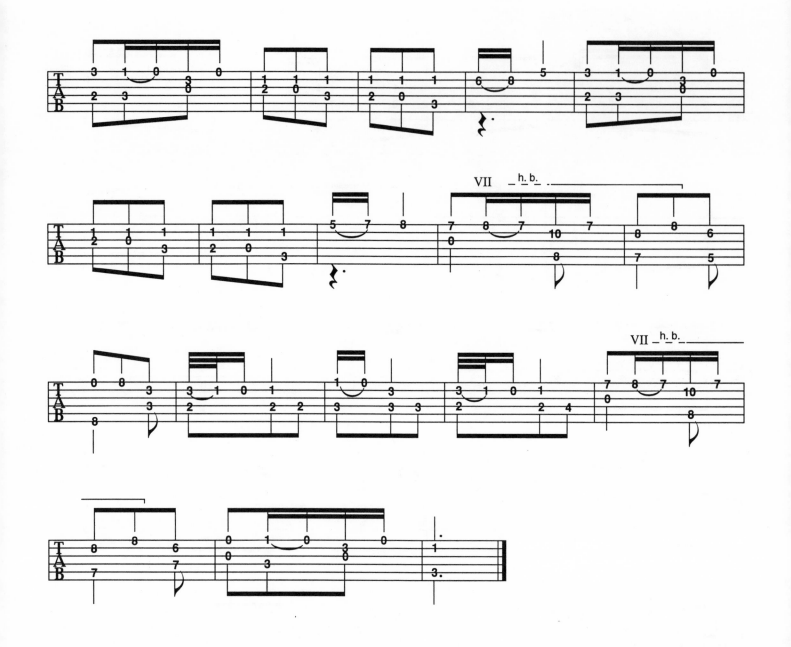

Fantasia in Em

George Philip Telemann
(arranged for guitar
by Stephen C. Siktberg)

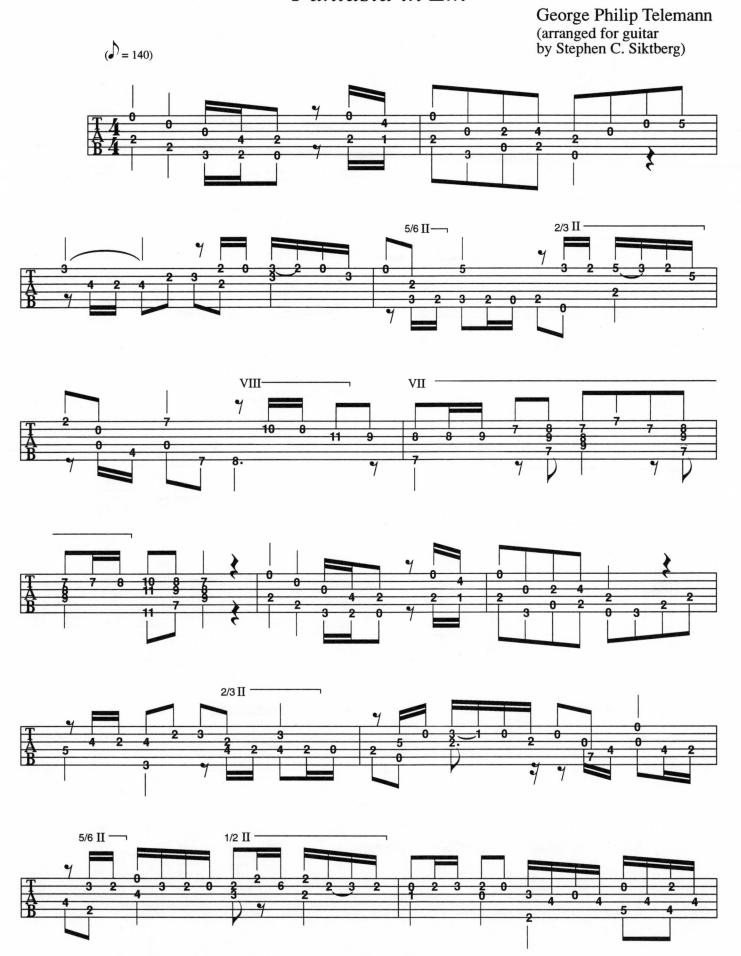

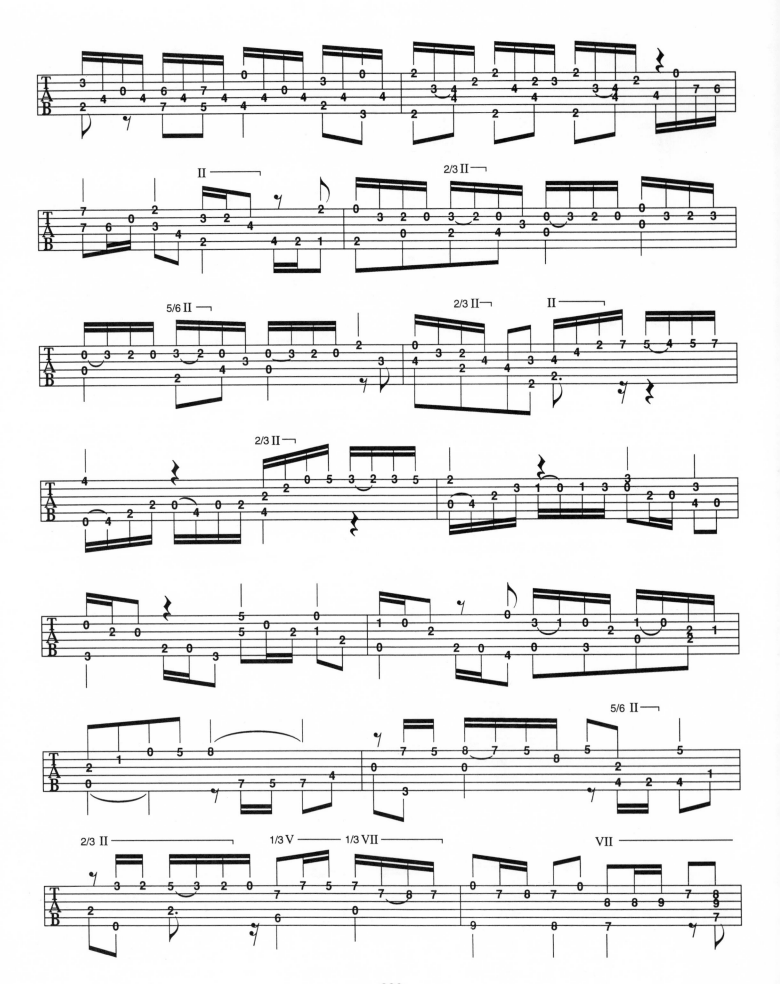

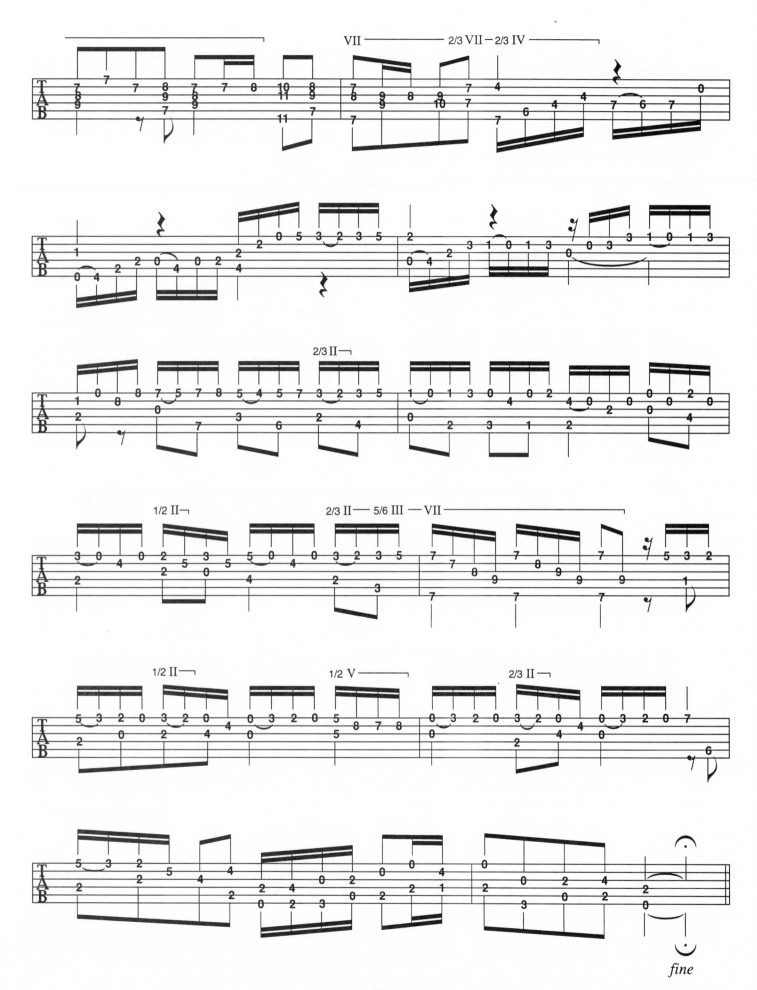

Adagio

(♪ = 116)

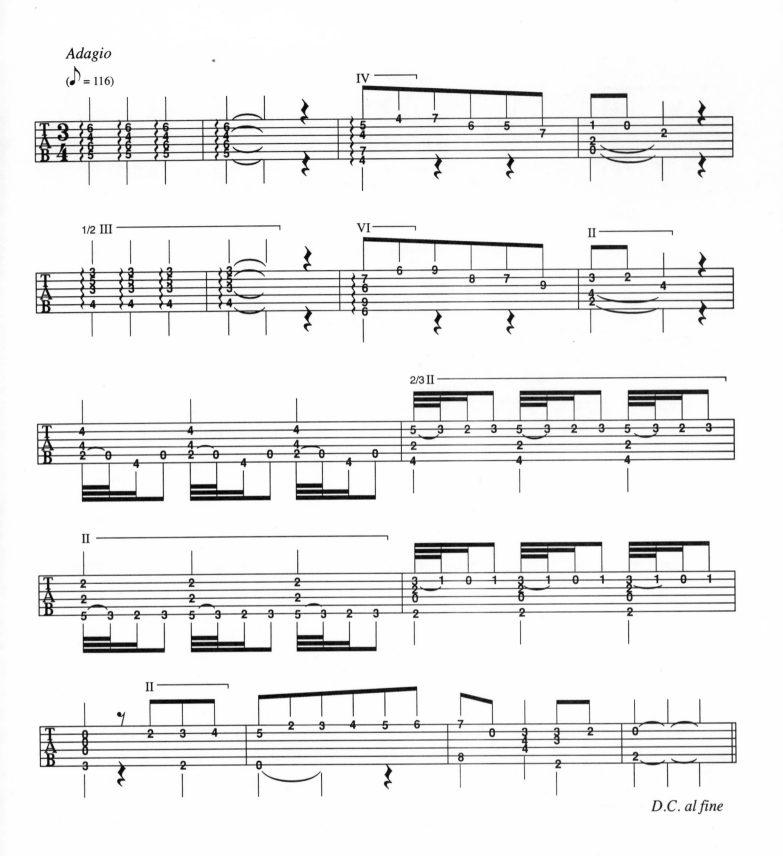

D.C. al fine

Sonatina in C

George Friedrich Handel
(arranged for guitar
by Stephen C. Siktberg)

Allemande

George Friedrich Handel
(arranged for guitar
by Stephen C. Siktberg)

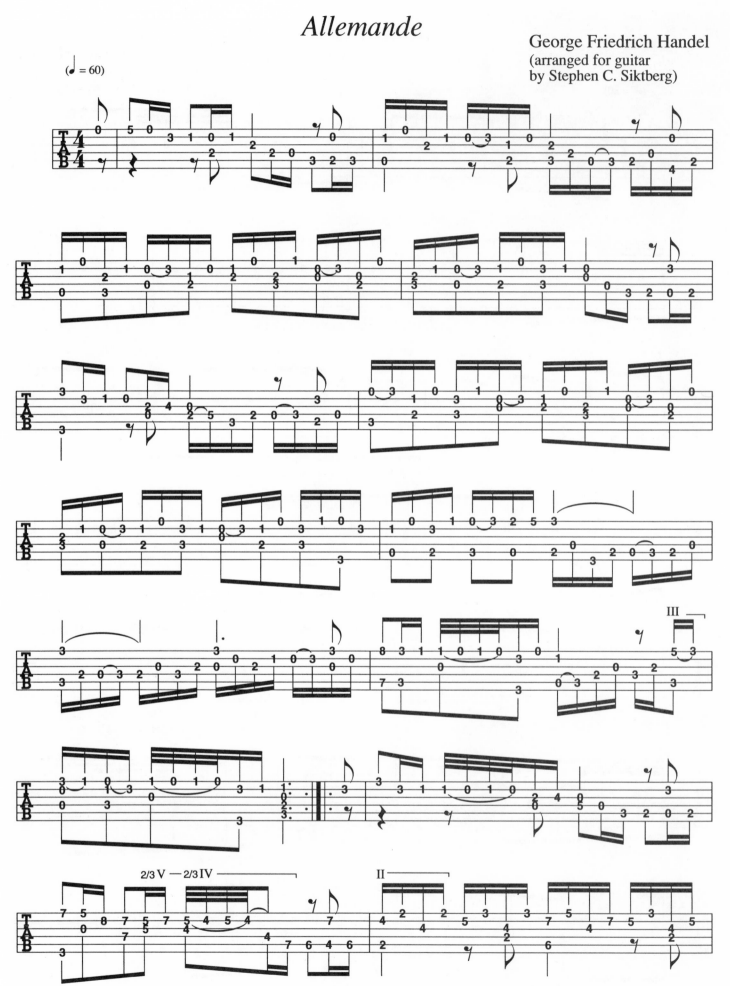

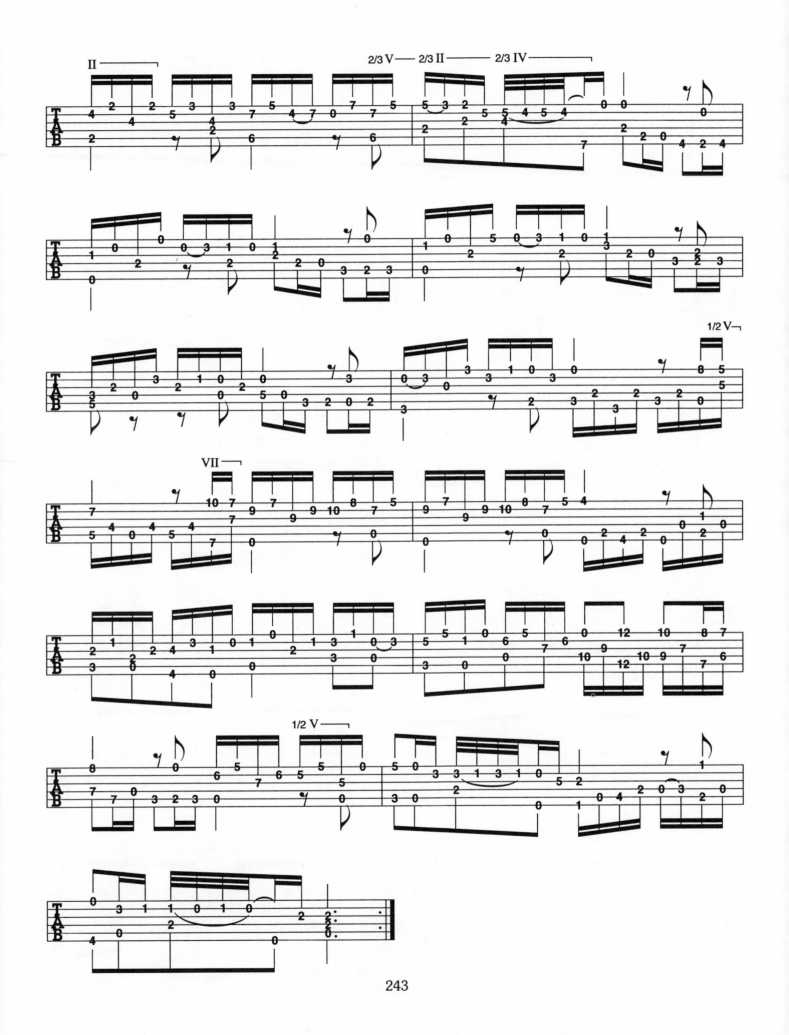

243

Sarabande
(with variations)

George Friedrich Handel
(arranged for guitar
by Stephen C. Siktberg)

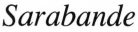

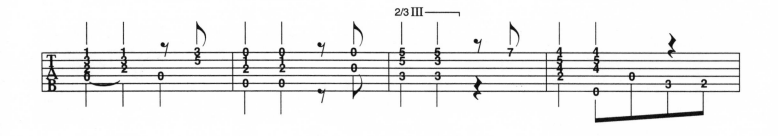

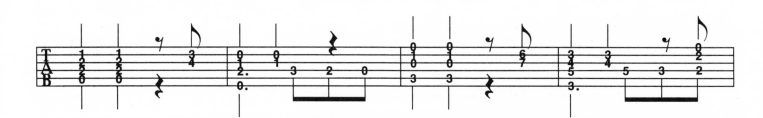

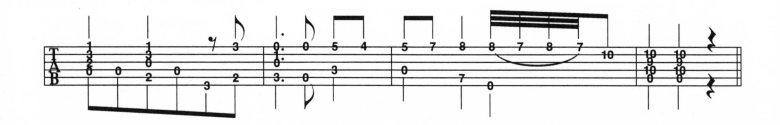

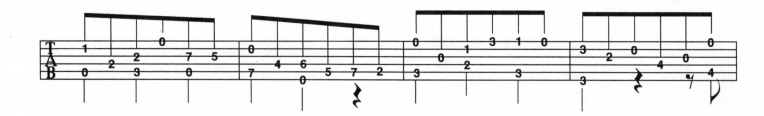

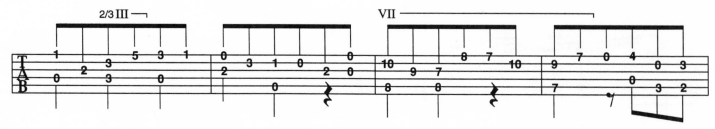

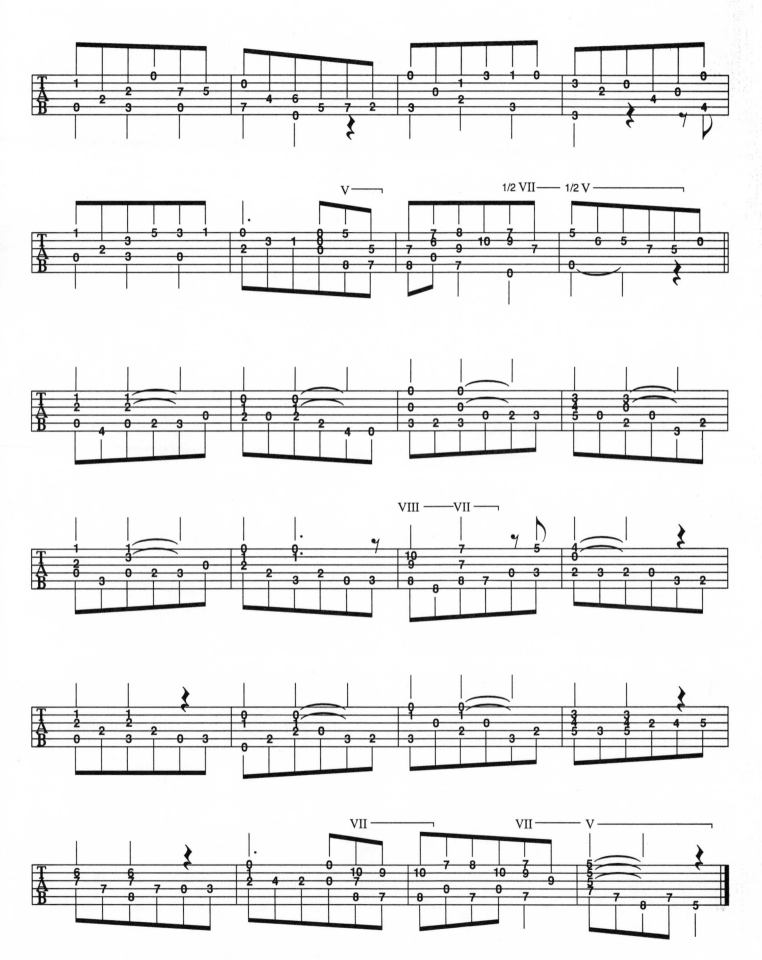

This page has been
left blank to avoid
awkward page turns

Allegro
(from Great Suite #7 for Harpsichord)

George Friedrich Handel
(arranged for guitar
by Stephen C. Siktberg)

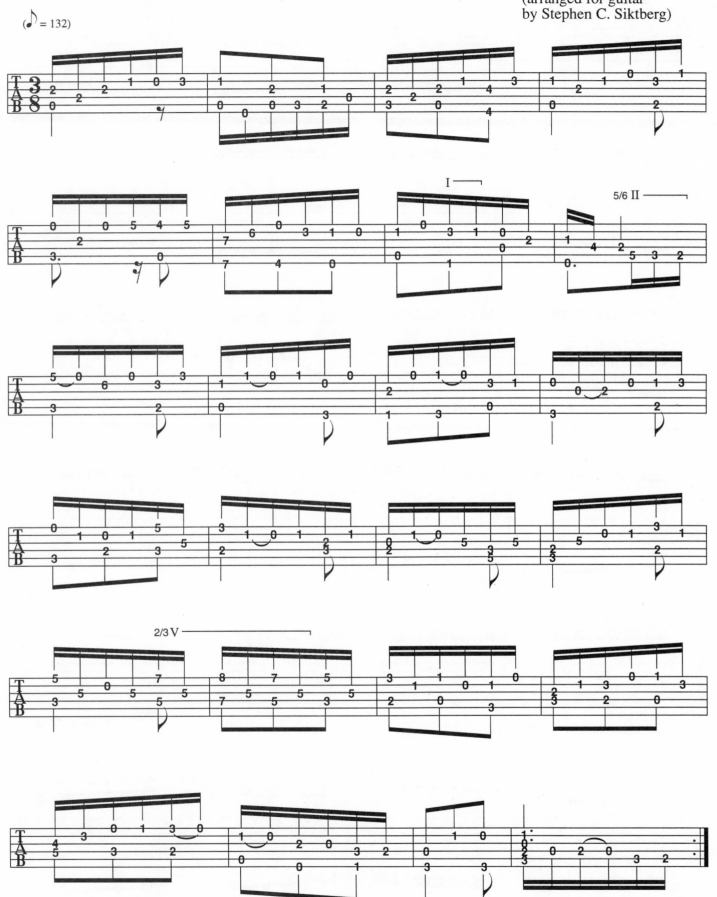

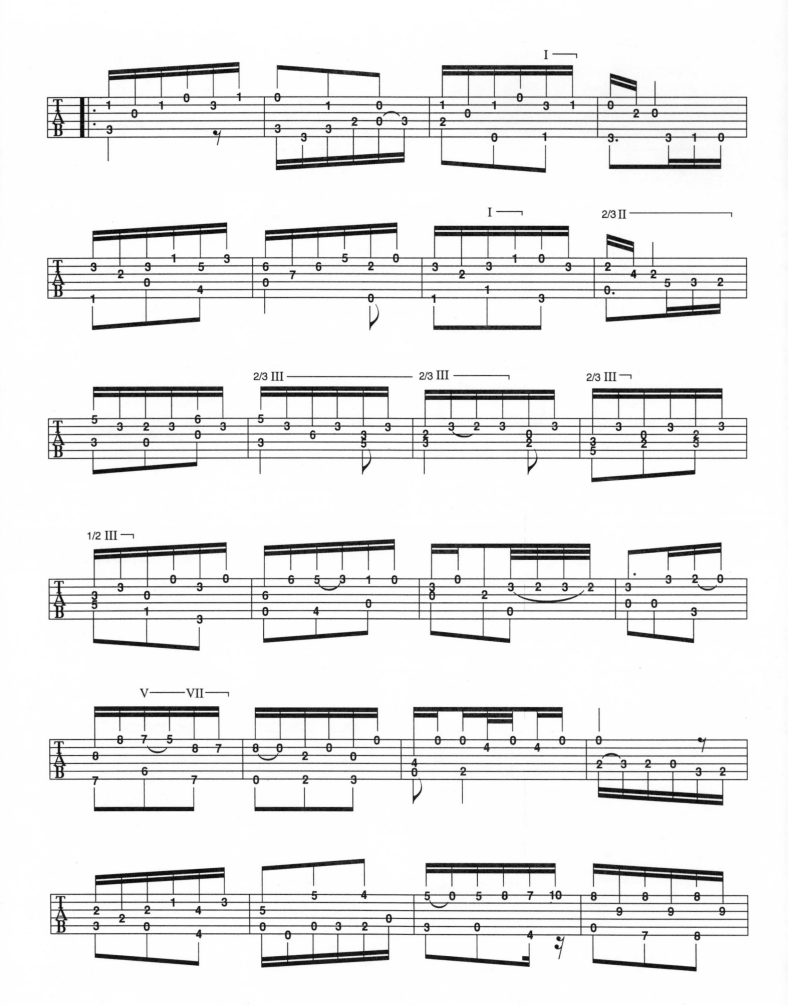

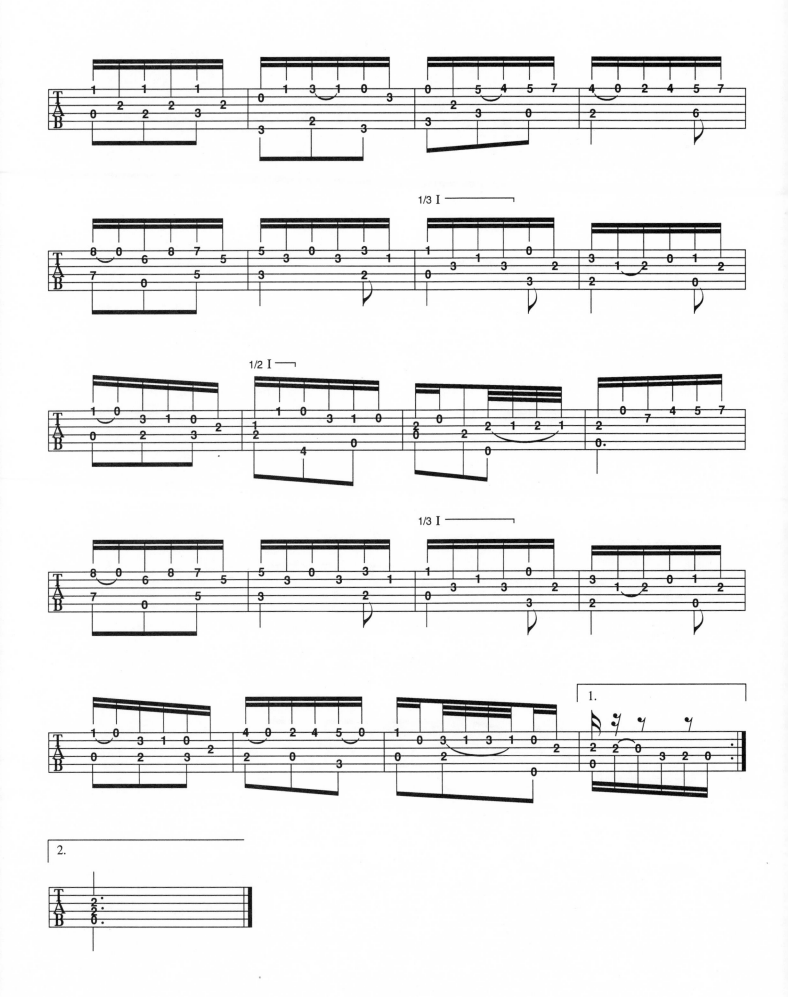

Sarabande
(from Great Suite #7)

George Friedrich Handel
(arranged for guitar
by Stephen C. Siktberg)

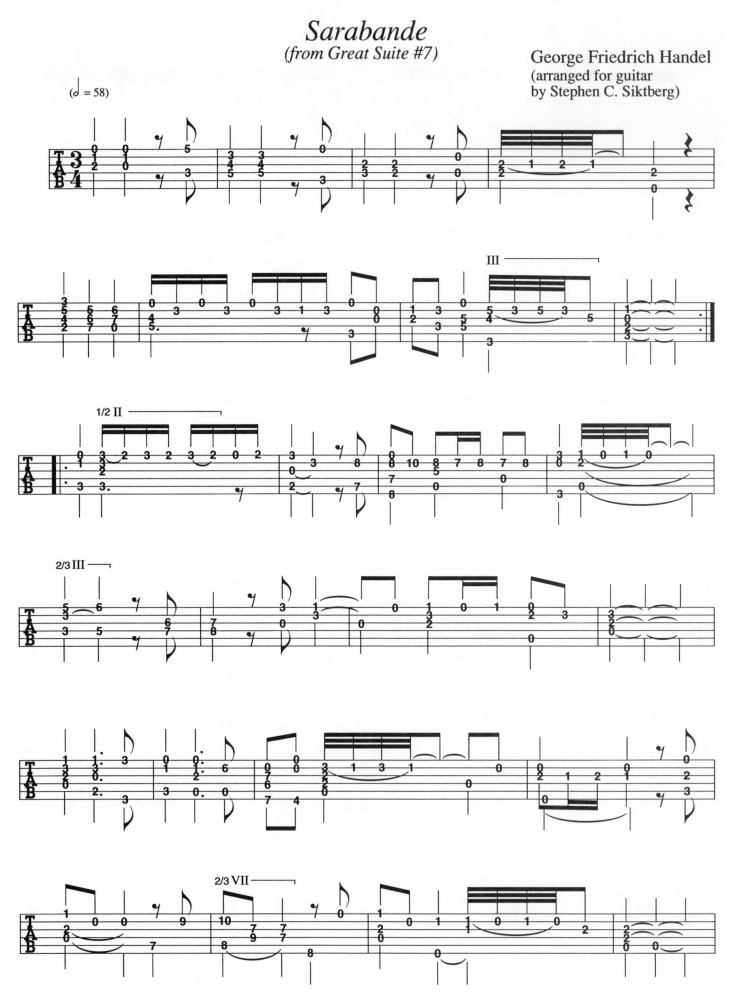

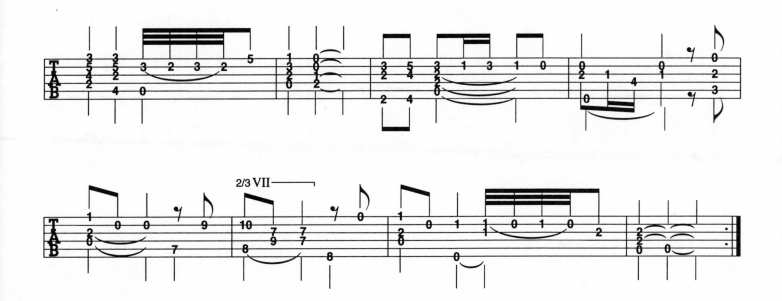

Passacaille
(from Great Suite #7)

George Friedrich Handel
(arranged for guitar
by Stephen C. Siktberg)

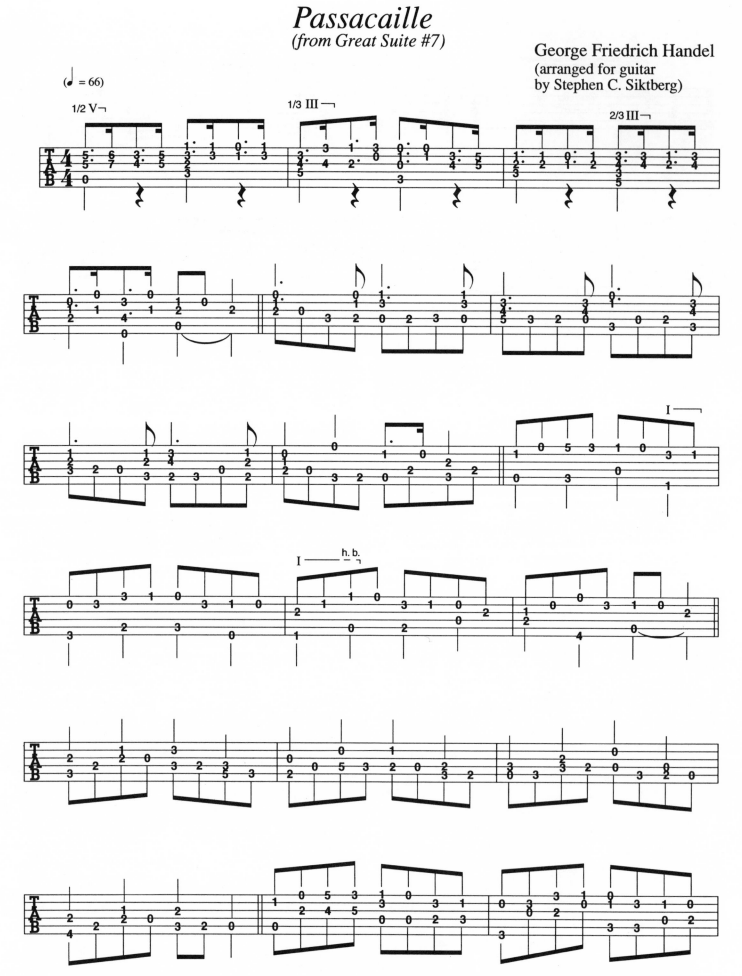

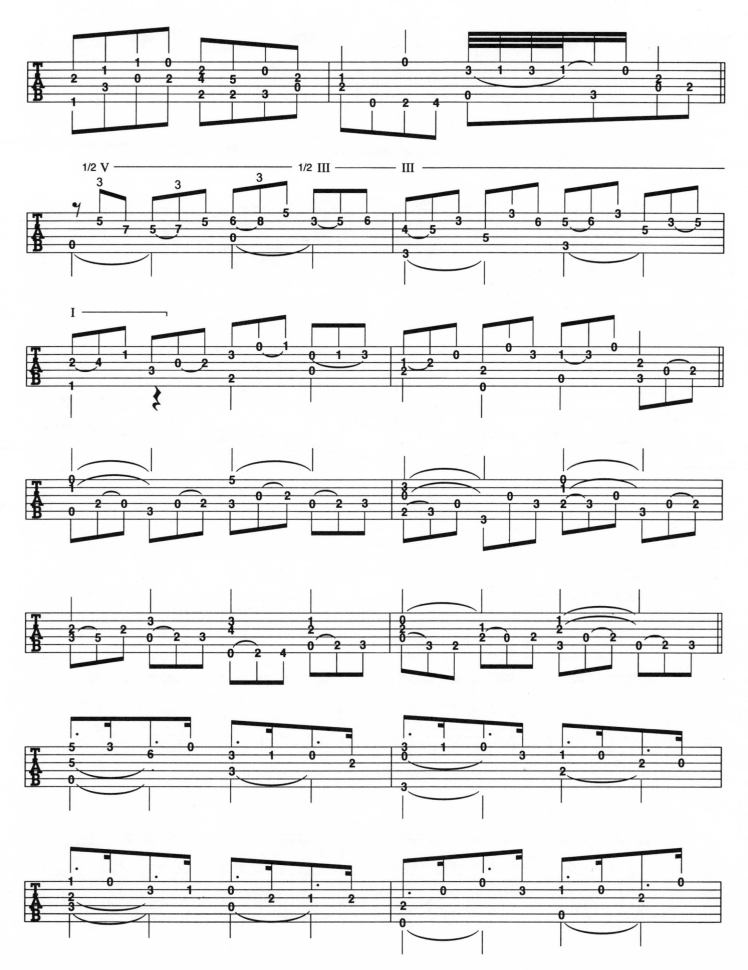

253

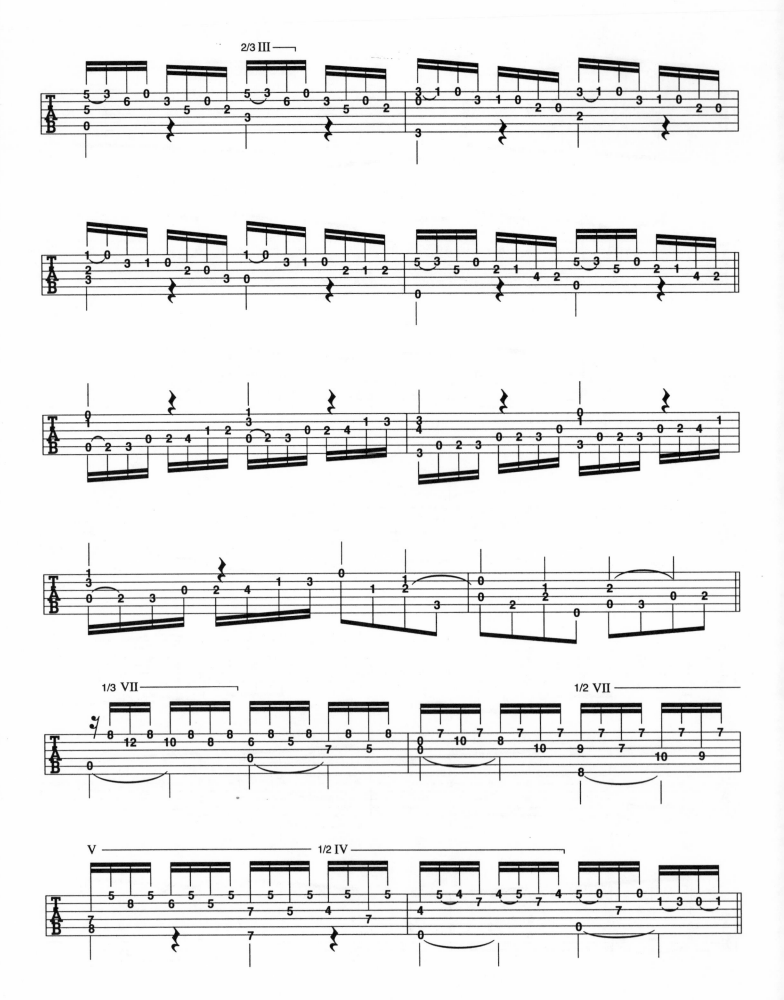

254

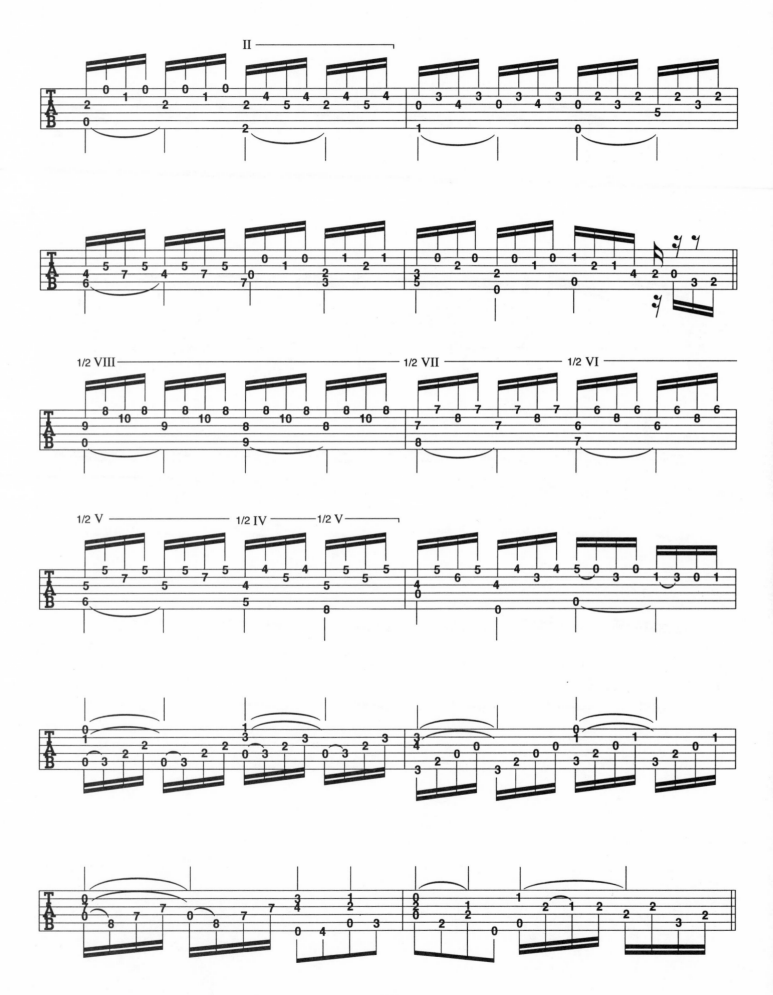

255

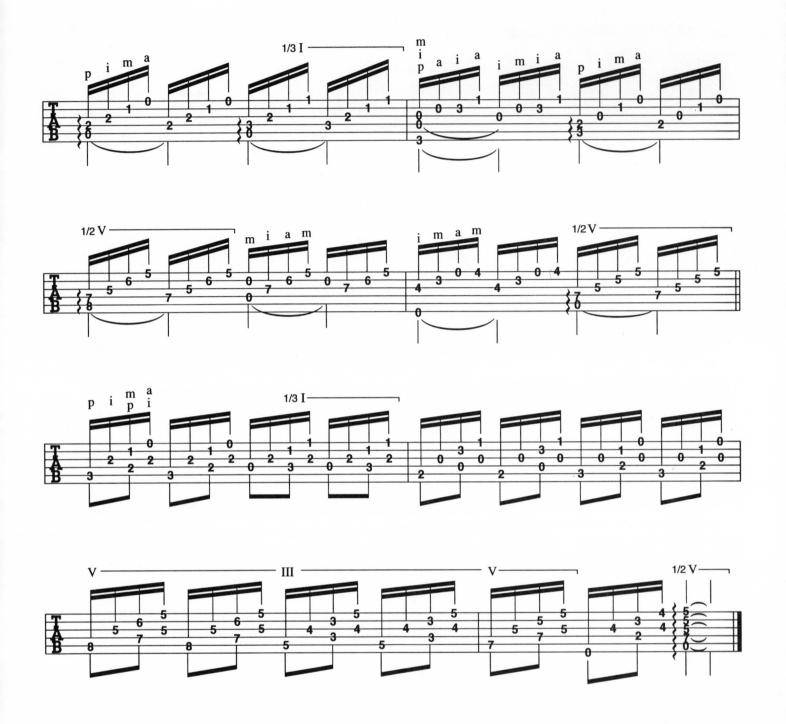

Allegro

(from Partita in G major for Harpsichord)

George Friedrich Handel
(arranged for guitar
by Stephen C. Siktberg)

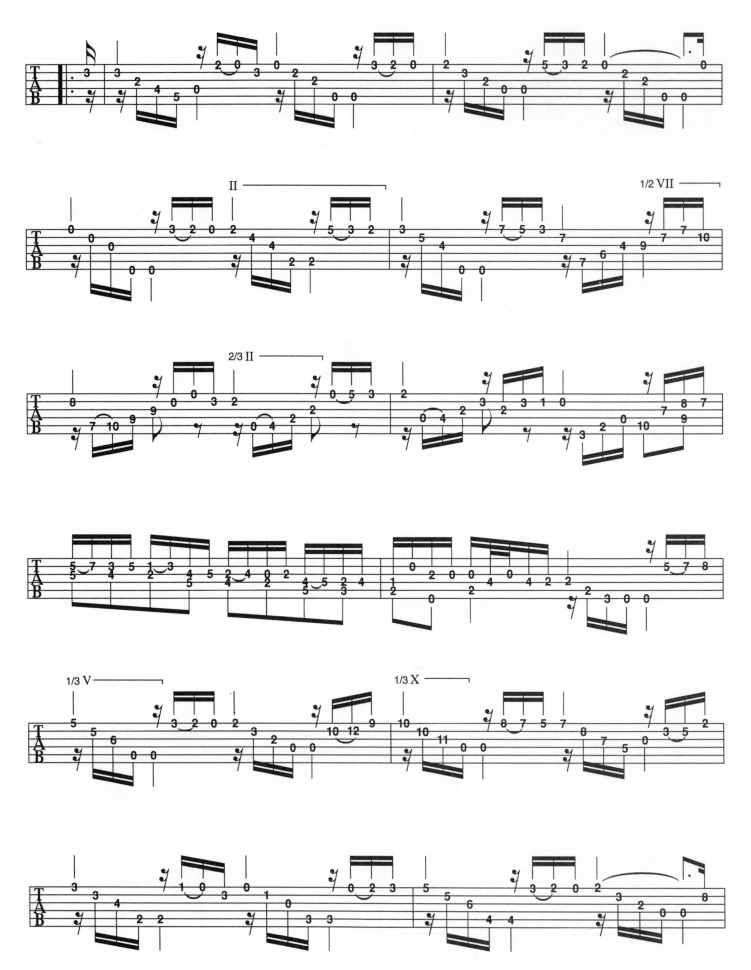

Courante

(from Partita in G major)

George Friedrich Handel
(arranged for guitar
by Stephen C. Siktberg)

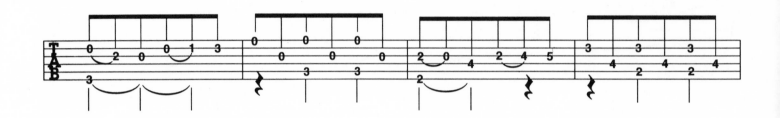

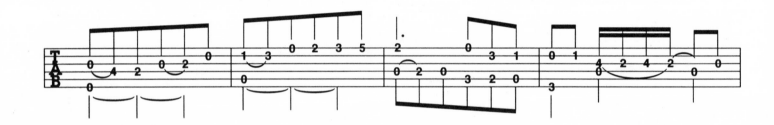

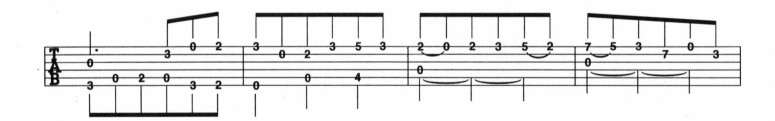

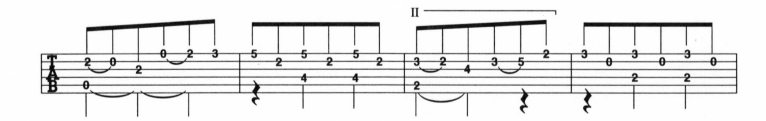

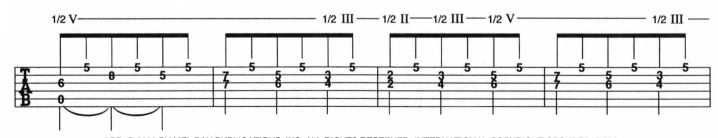

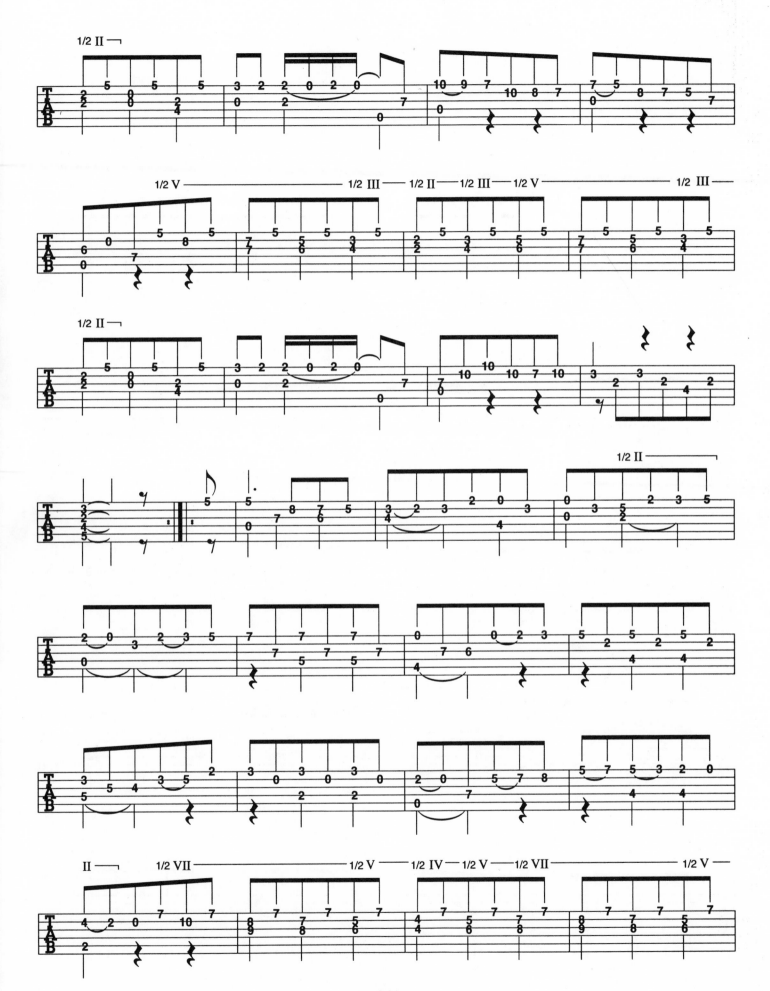

261

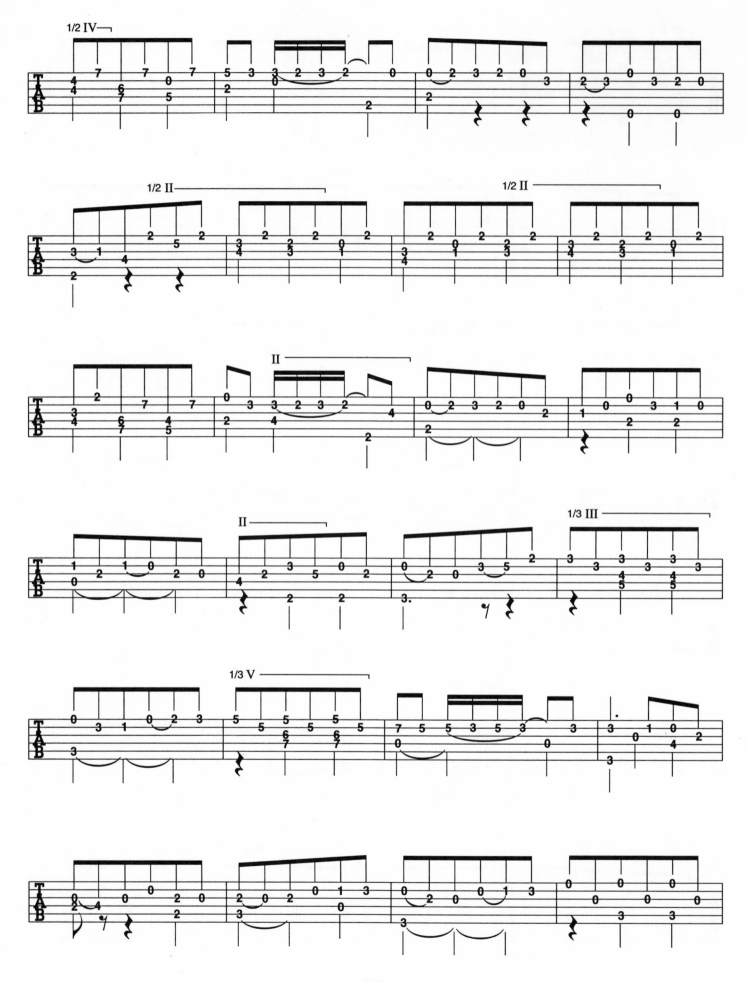

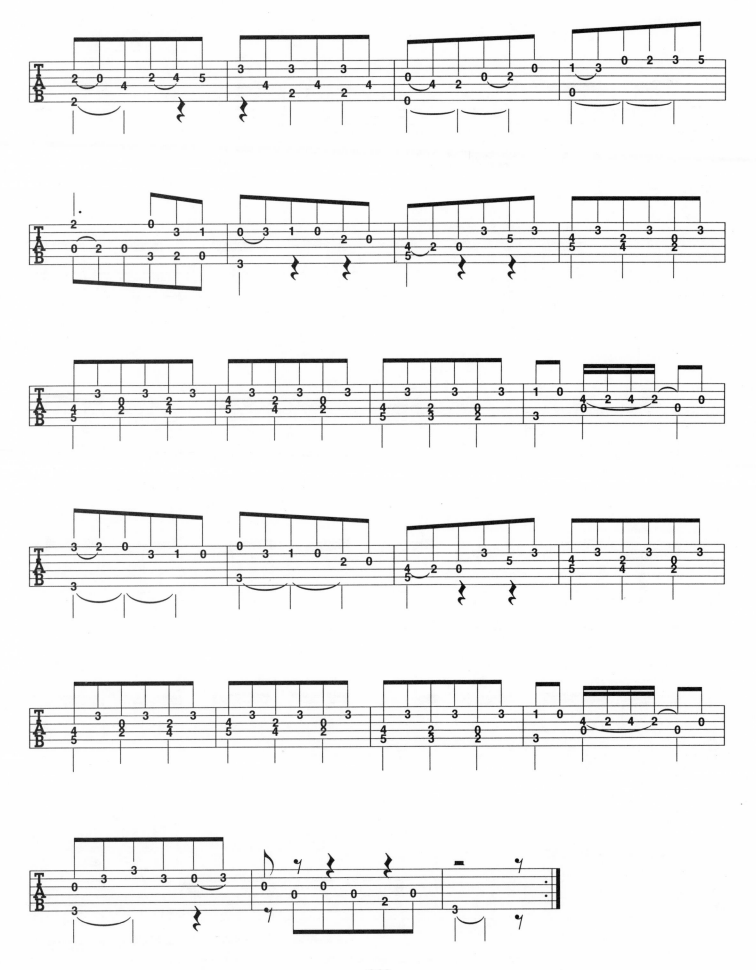

263

Sonata in C

Capo 3rd fret

George Friedrich Handel
(arranged for guitar
by Stephen C. Siktberg)

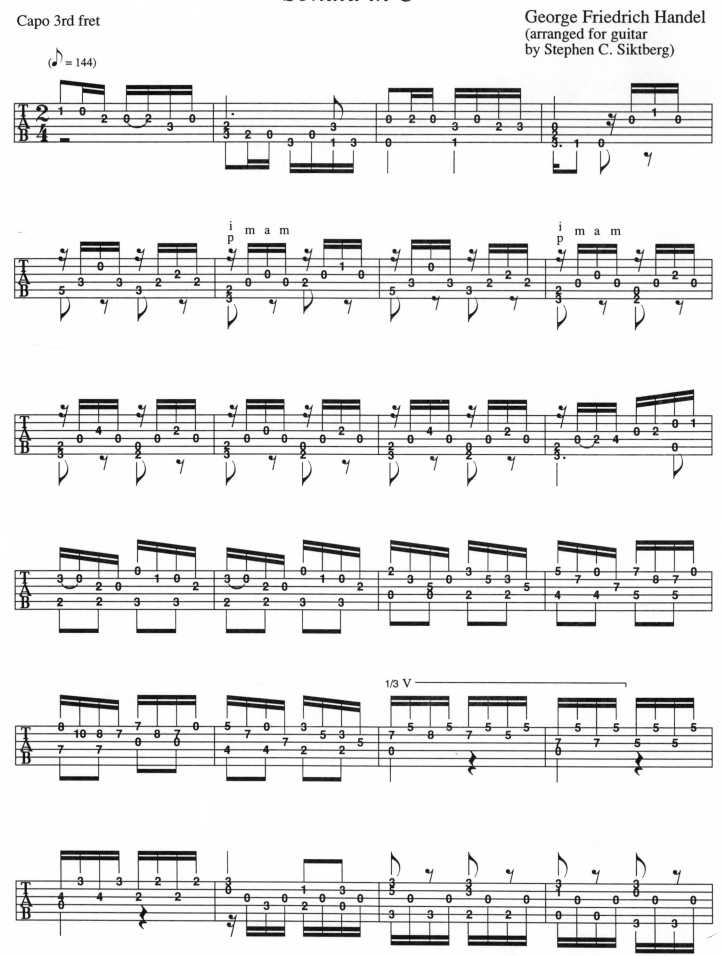

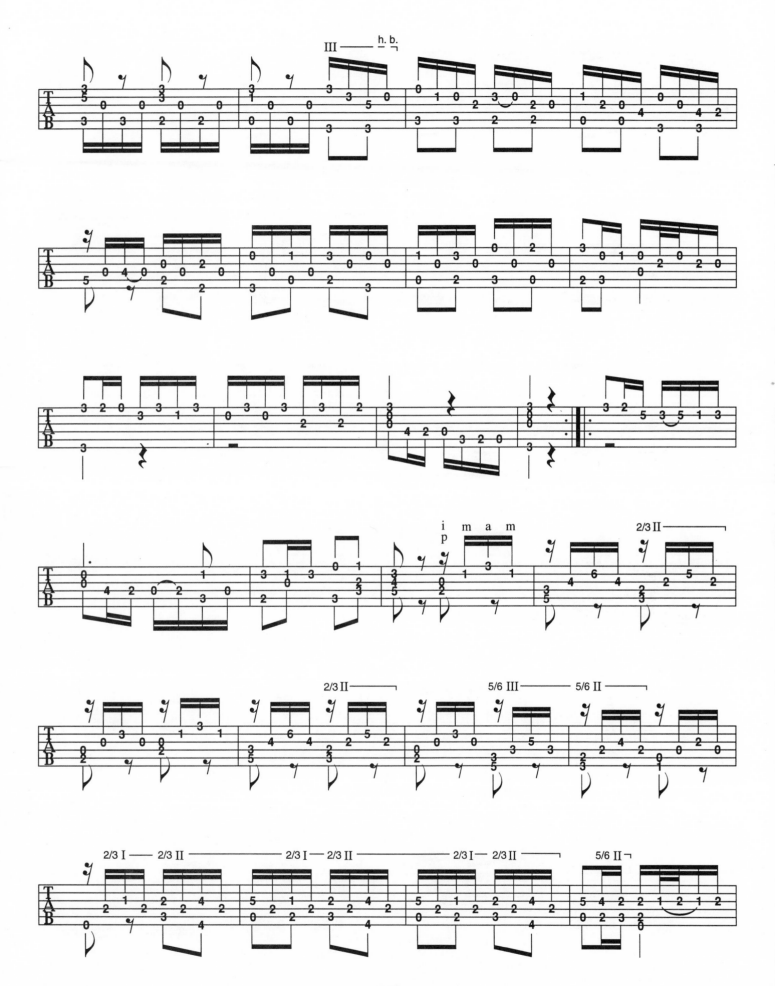

265

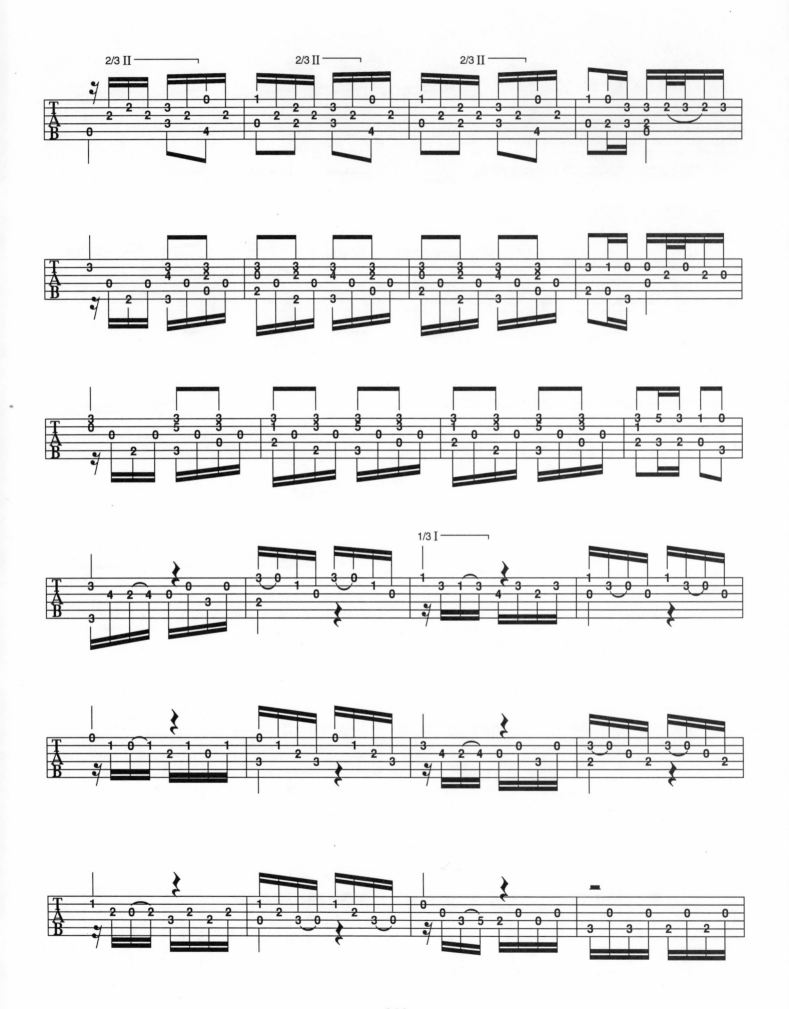

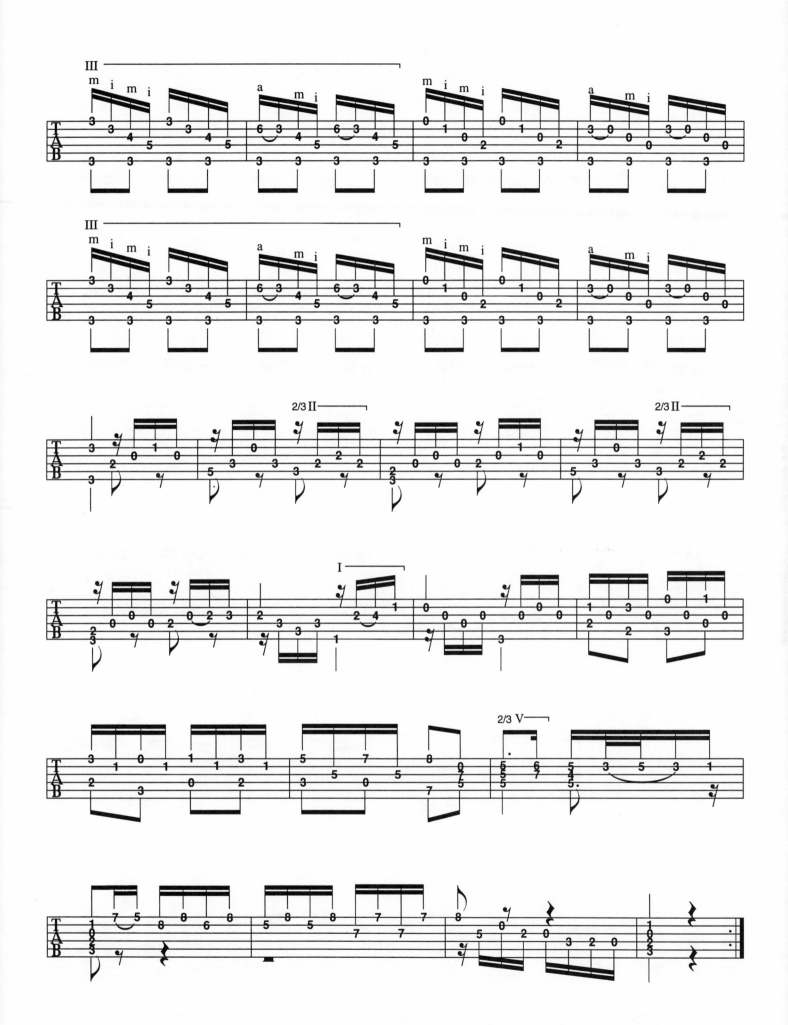

267

Prelude
(from Suite #1 for Violoncello)

J. S. Bach
(arranged for guitar
by Stephen C. Siktberg)

($\bullet$ = 68)

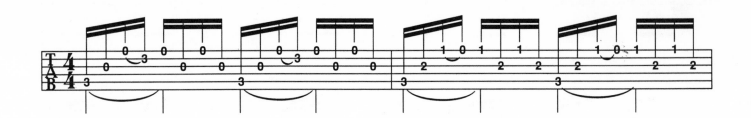

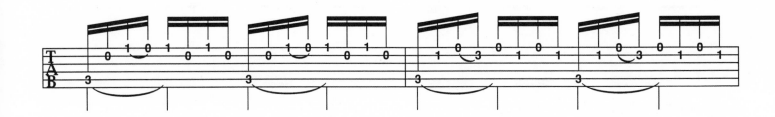

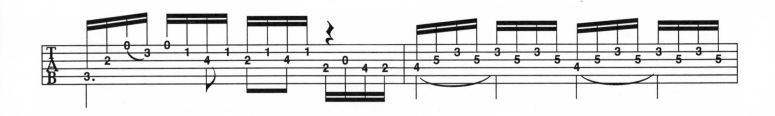

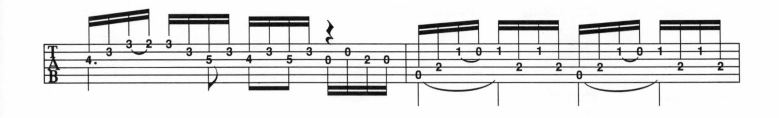

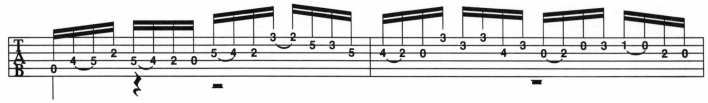

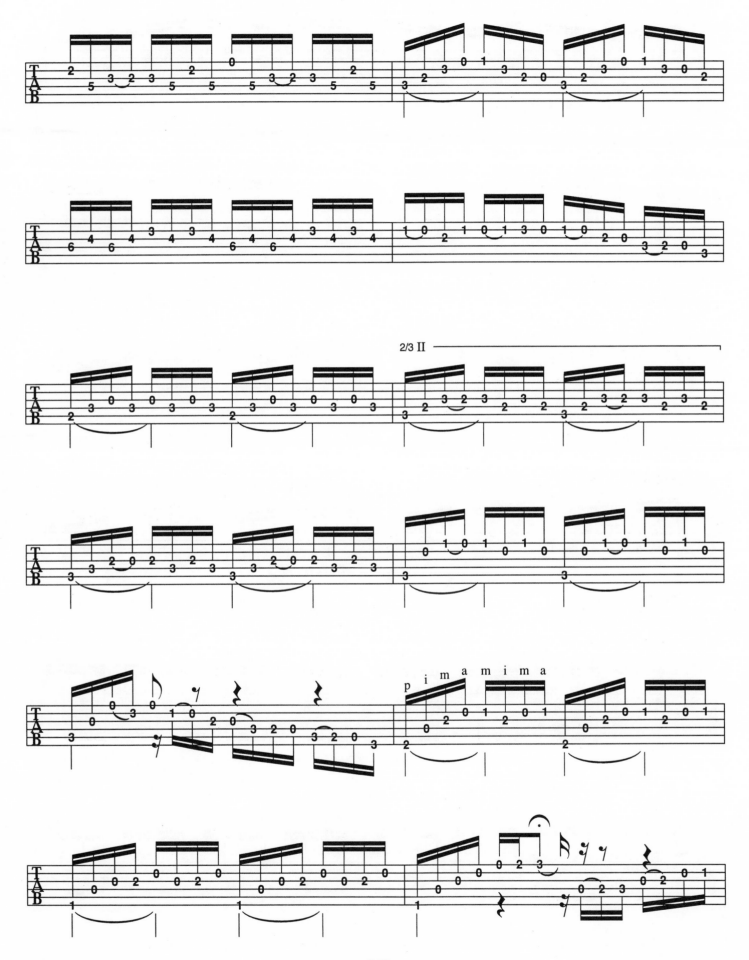

269

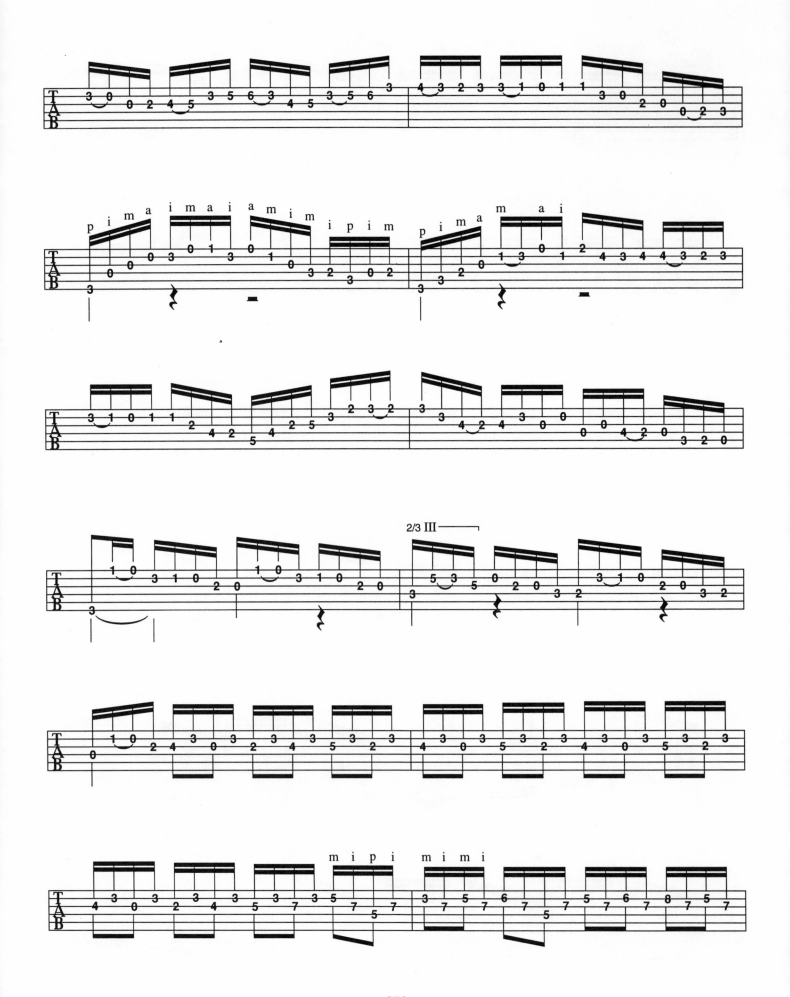

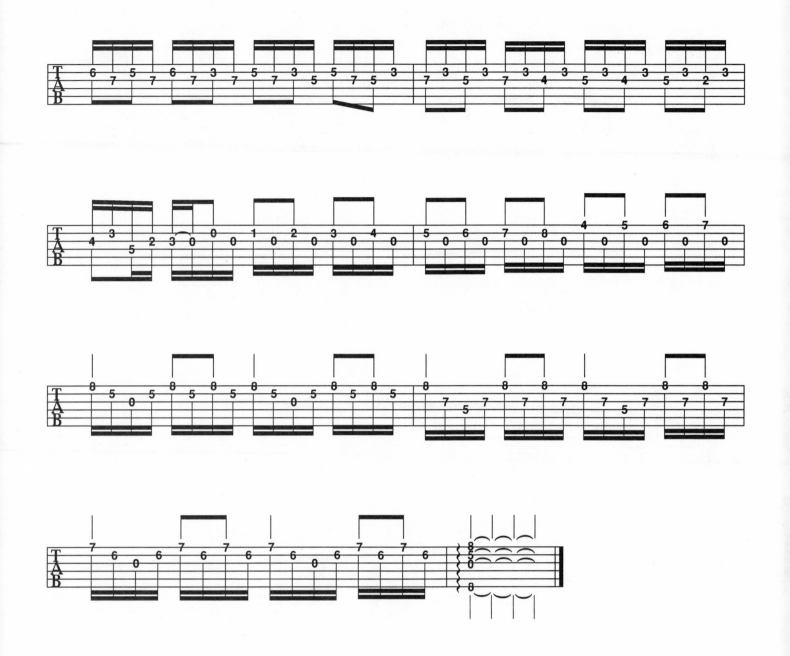

Menuet 1
(from Suite #1 for Violoncello)

J. S. Bach
(arranged for guitar
by Stephen C. Siktberg)

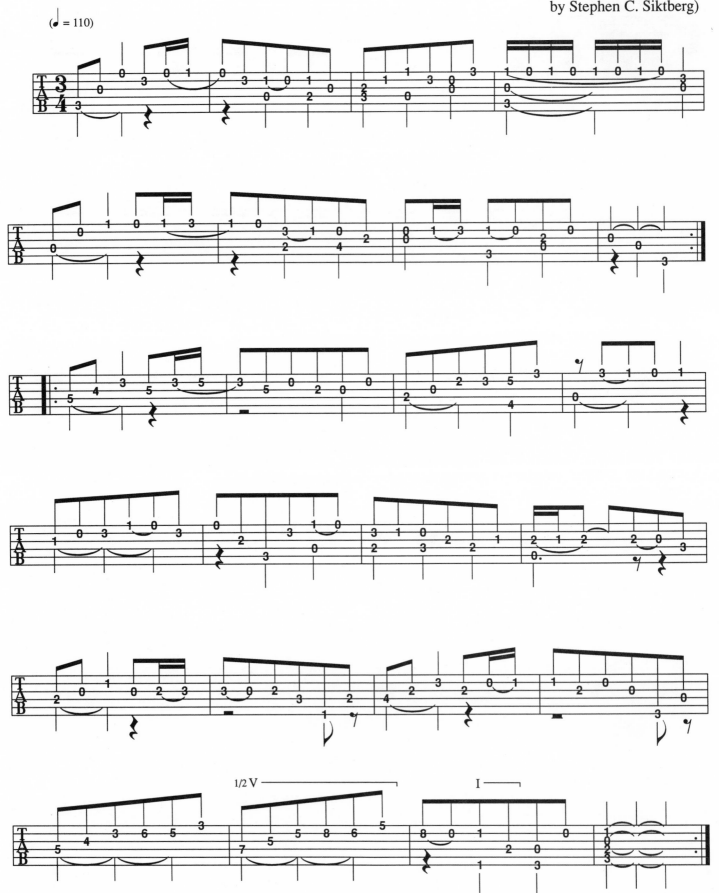

Menuet 2
(from Suite #1 for Violoncello)

J. S. Bach
(arranged for guitar
by Stephen C. Siktberg)

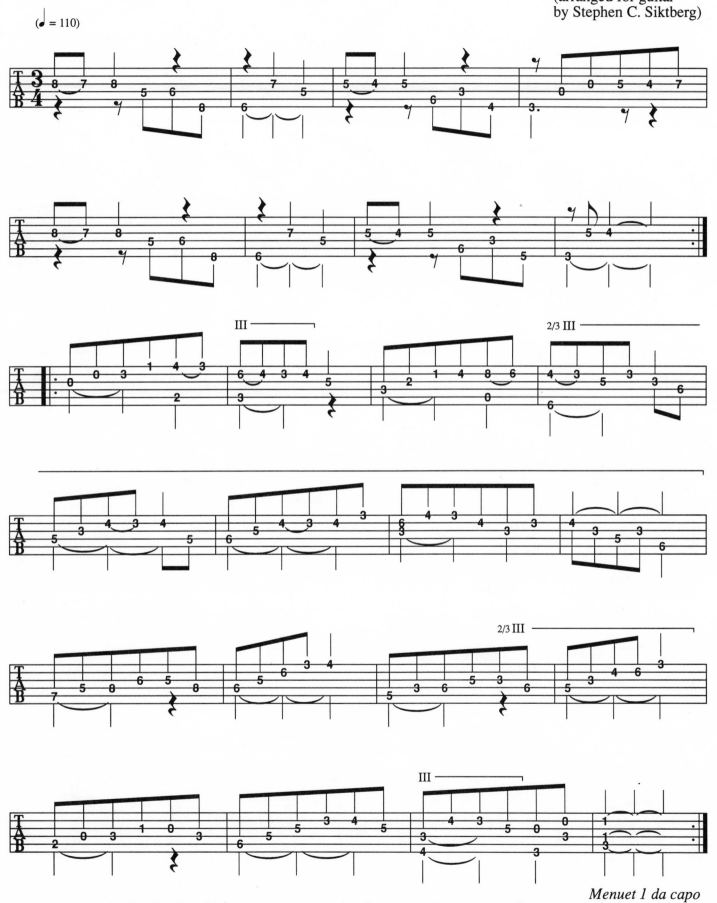

Menuet 1 da capo

Gigue

(from Suite #1 for Violoncello)

J. S. Bach
(arranged for guitar
by Stephen C. Siktberg)

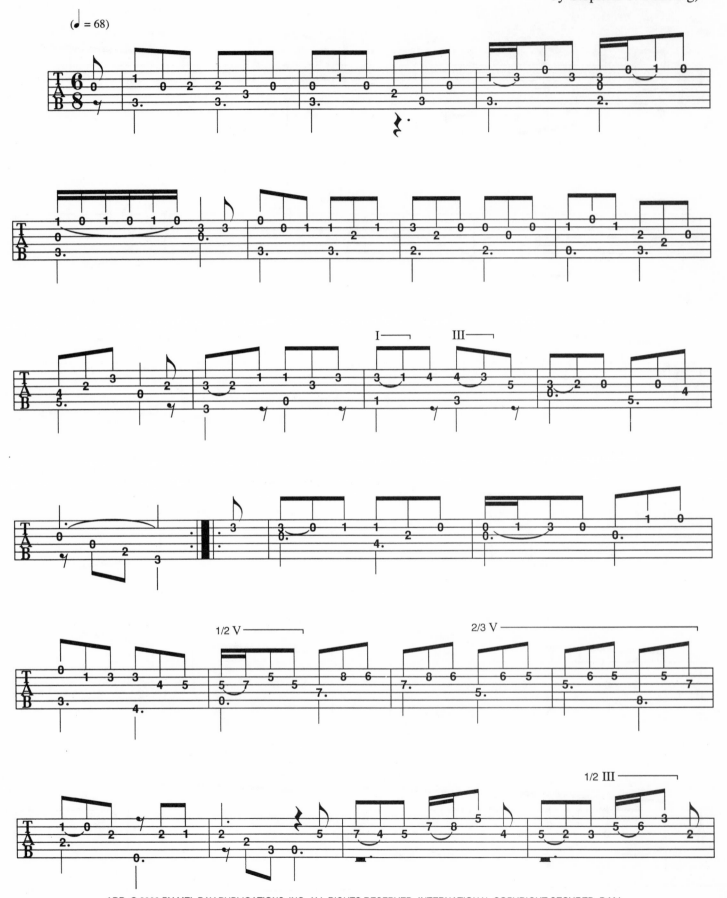

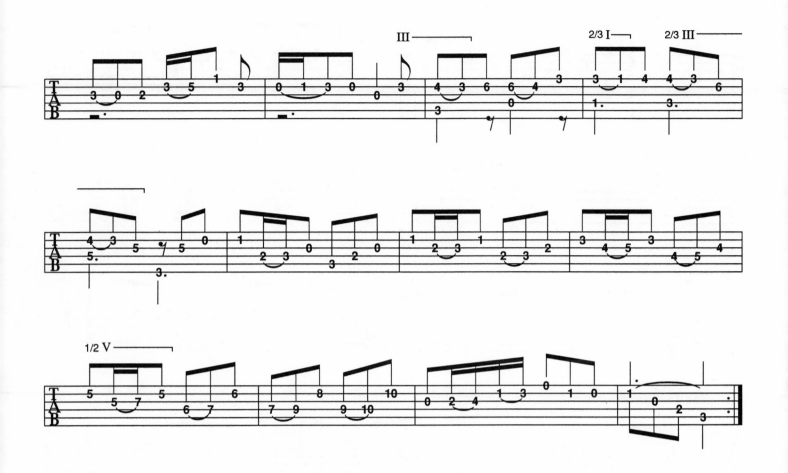

Gavotte 1
(from Suite #6 for Violoncello)

J. S. Bach
(arranged for guitar
by Stephen C. Siktberg)

Gavotte 2
(from Suite #6 for Violoncello)

J. S. Bach
(arranged for guitar
by Stephen C. Siktberg)

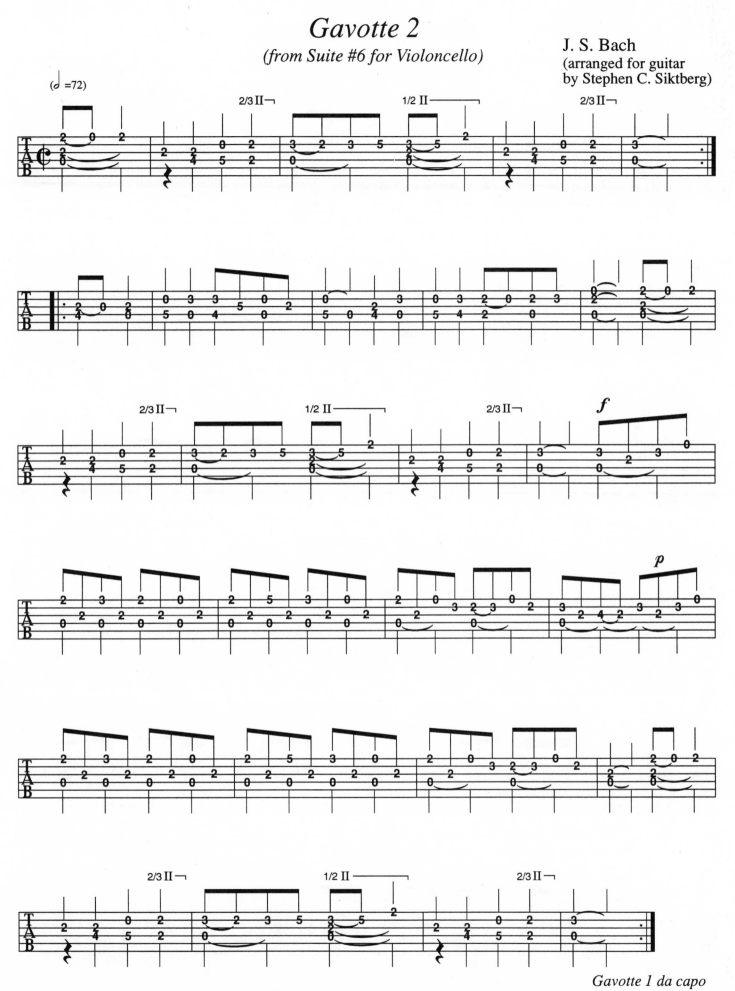

Gavotte 1 da capo

Gavotte en Rondeau
(from Partita #3 for Violin)

J. S. Bach
(arranged for guitar
by Stephen C. Siktberg)

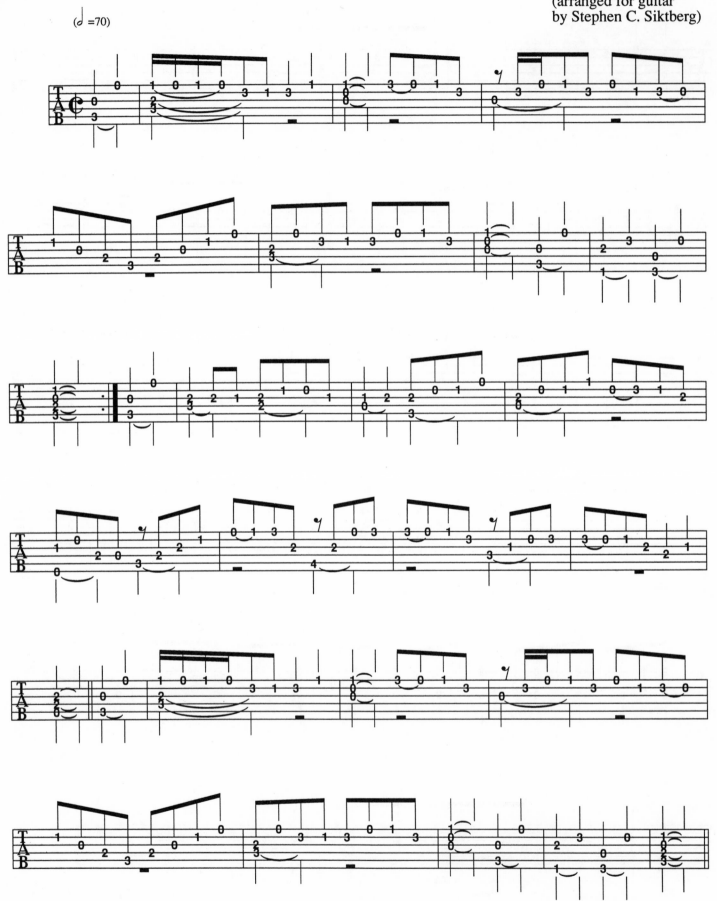

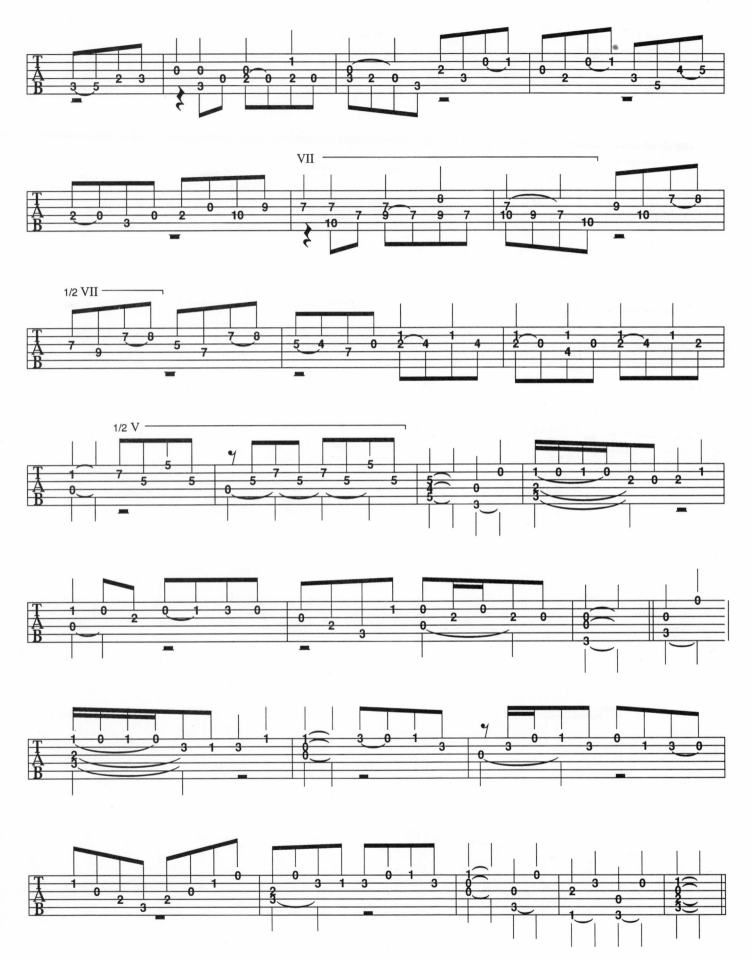

279

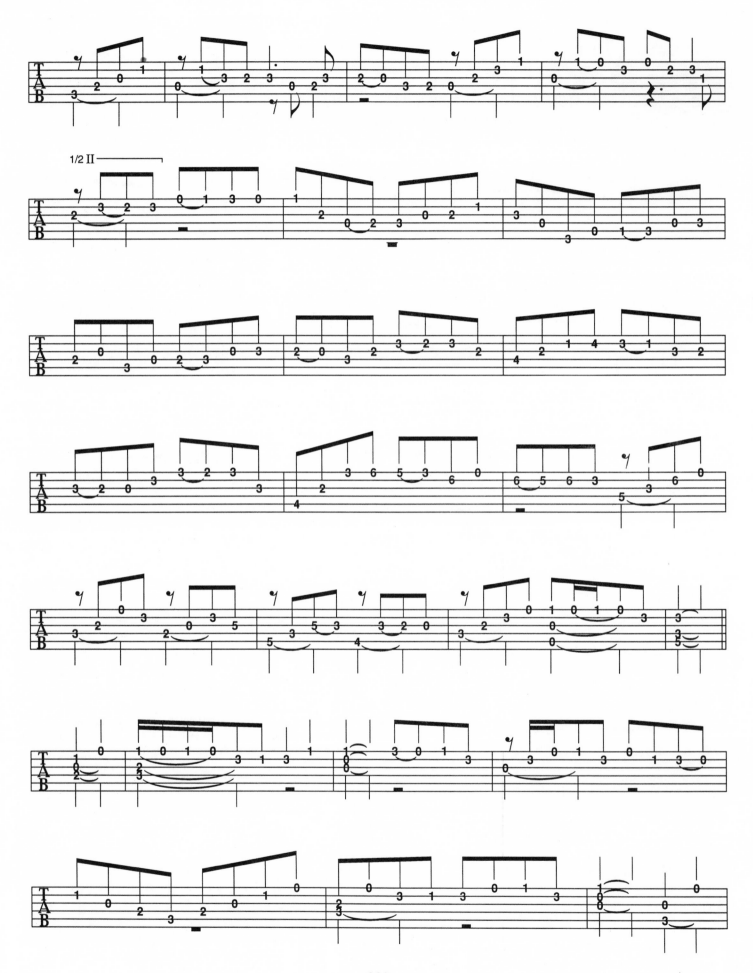

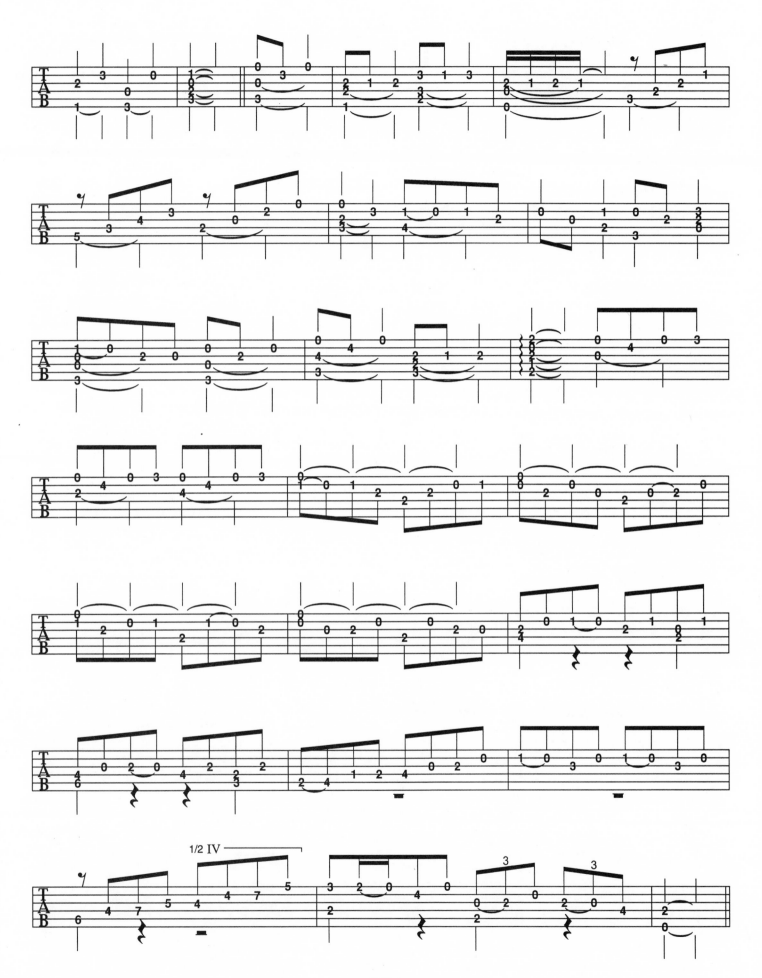

281

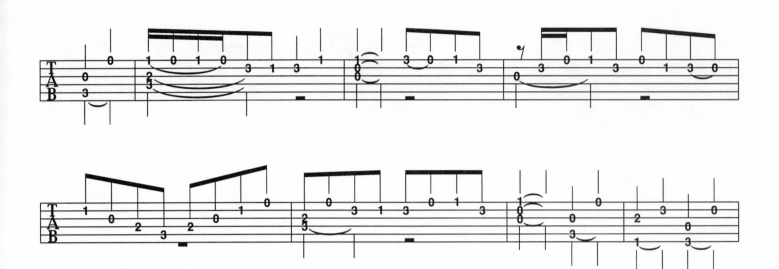

Menuet 1
(from Partita #3 for Violin)

J. S. Bach
(arranged for guitar
by Stephen C. Siktberg)

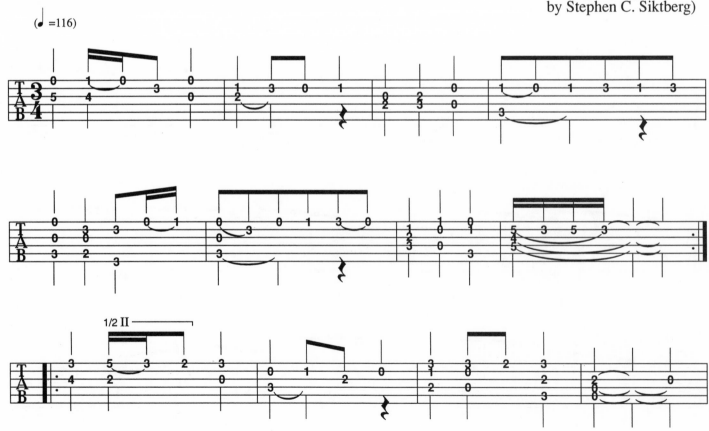

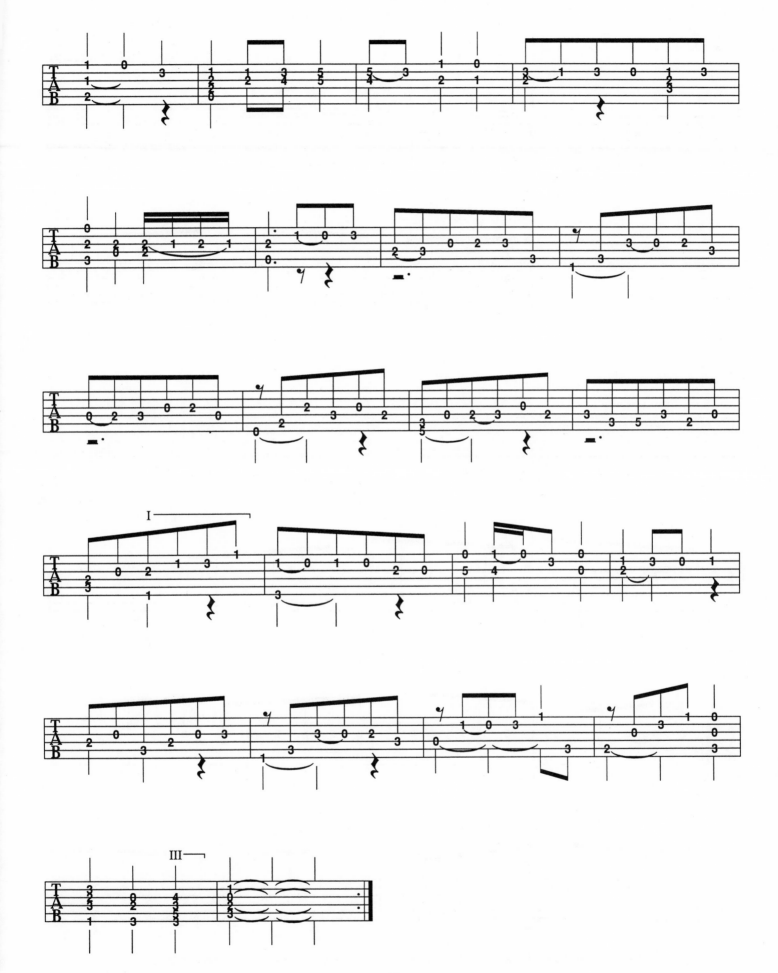

Menuet 2
(from Partita #3 for Violin)

J. S. Bach

(arranged for guitar
by Stephen C. Siktberg)

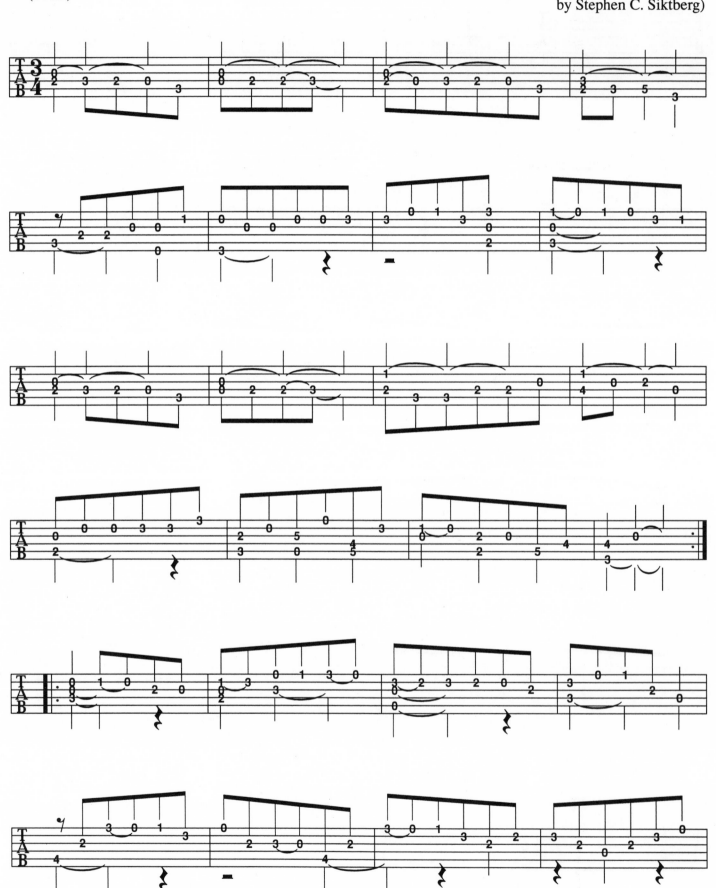

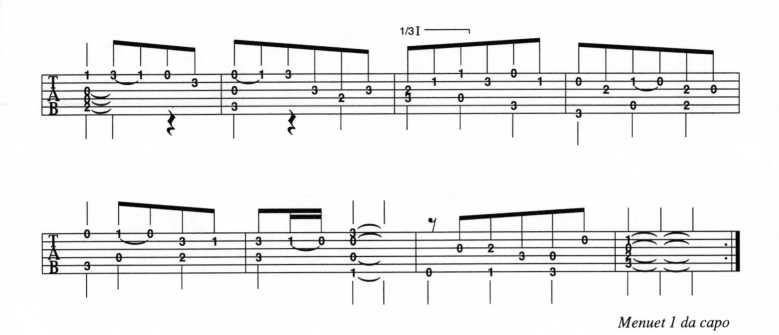

Menuet 1 da capo

Bourée
(from Partita #3 for Violin)

J. S. Bach
(arranged for guitar
by Stephen C. Siktberg)

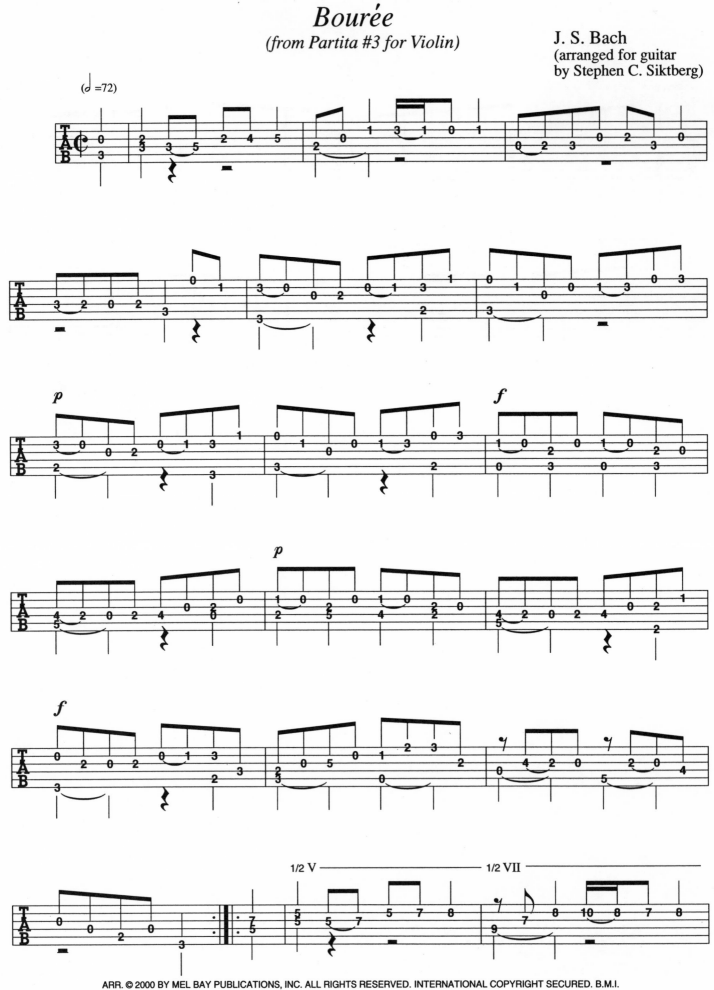

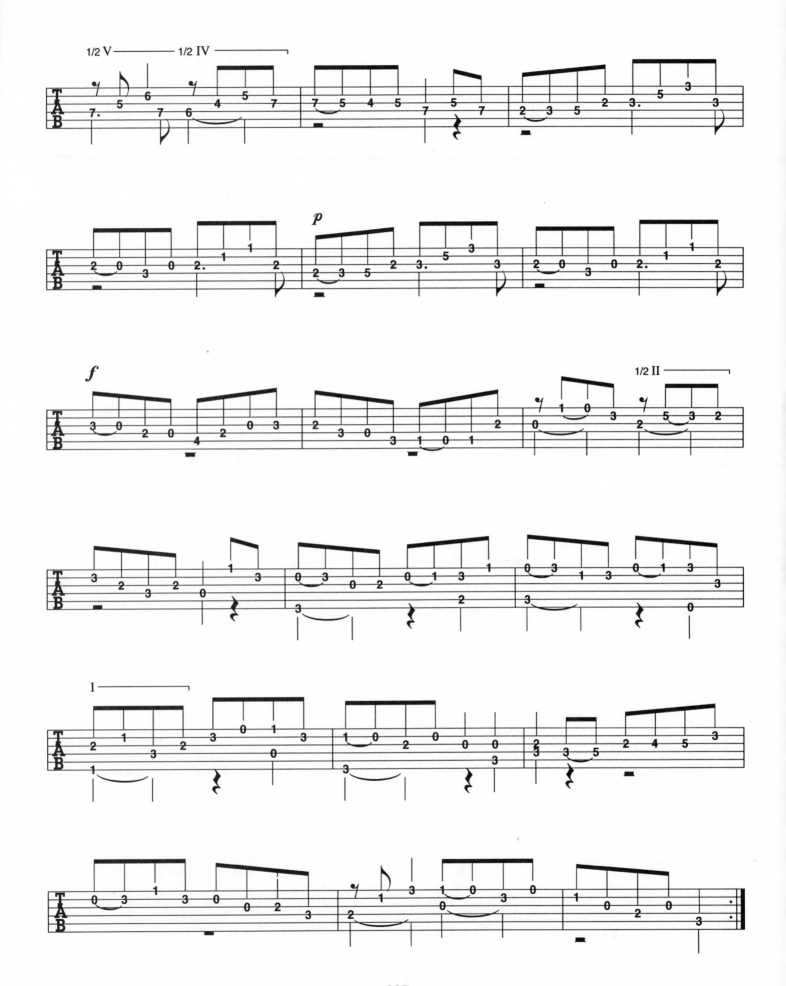

Sarabande & Double
(from Partita #1 for Violin)

J. S. Bach
(arranged for guitar
by Stephen C. Siktberg)

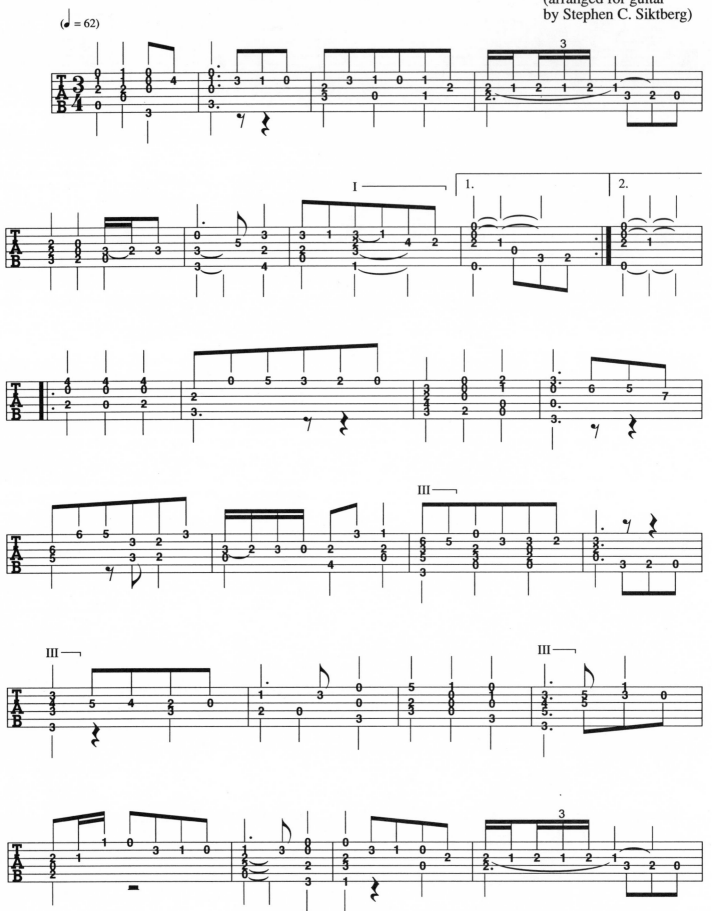

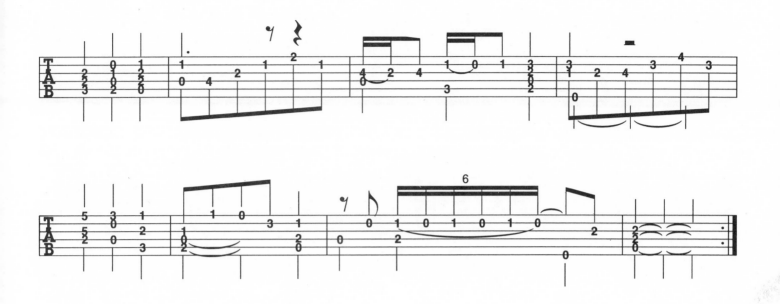

Double

$(\quarter. =100)$

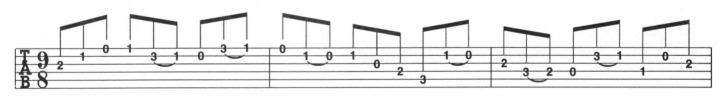

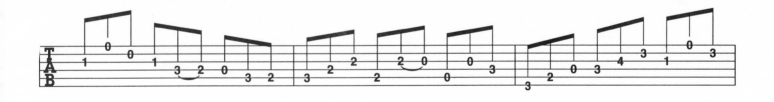

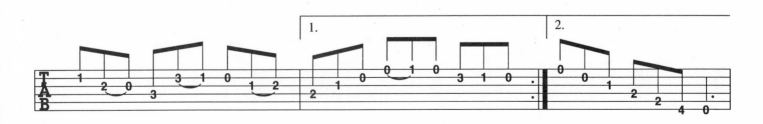

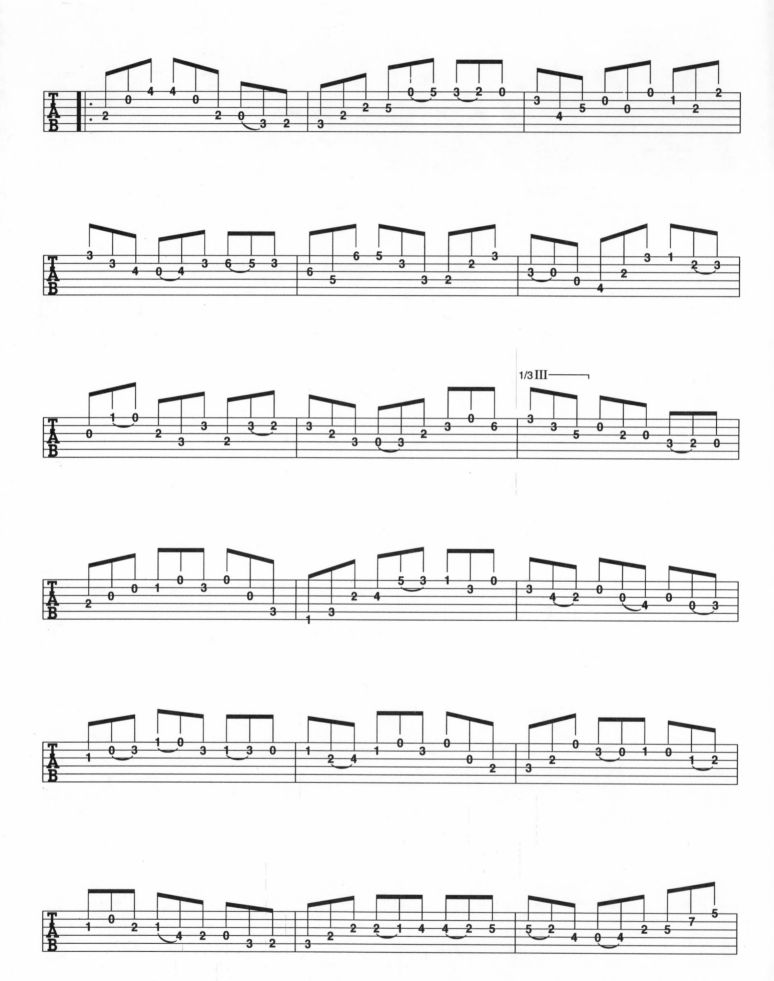

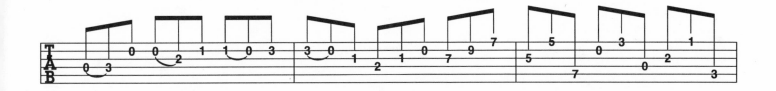

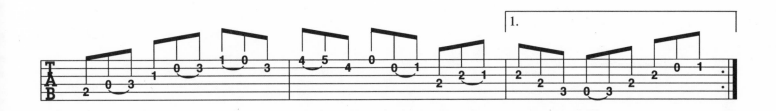

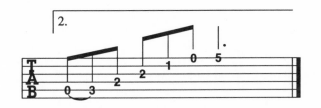

Tempo di Bourée
(from Partita #1 for Violin)

J. S. Bach
(arranged for guitar
by Stephen C. Siktberg)

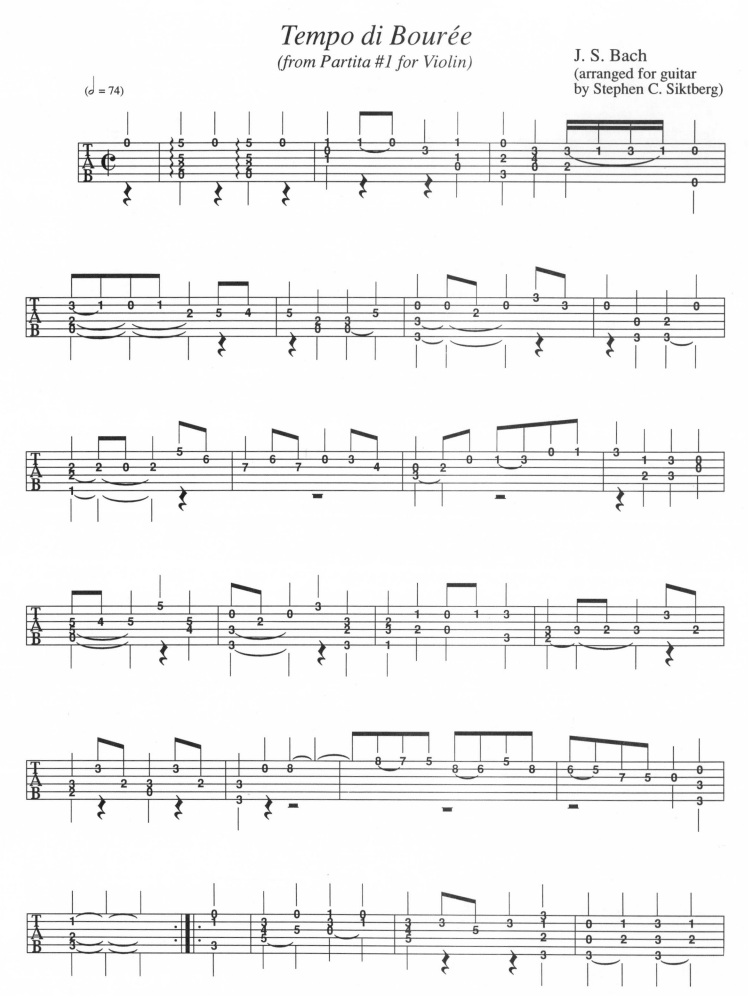

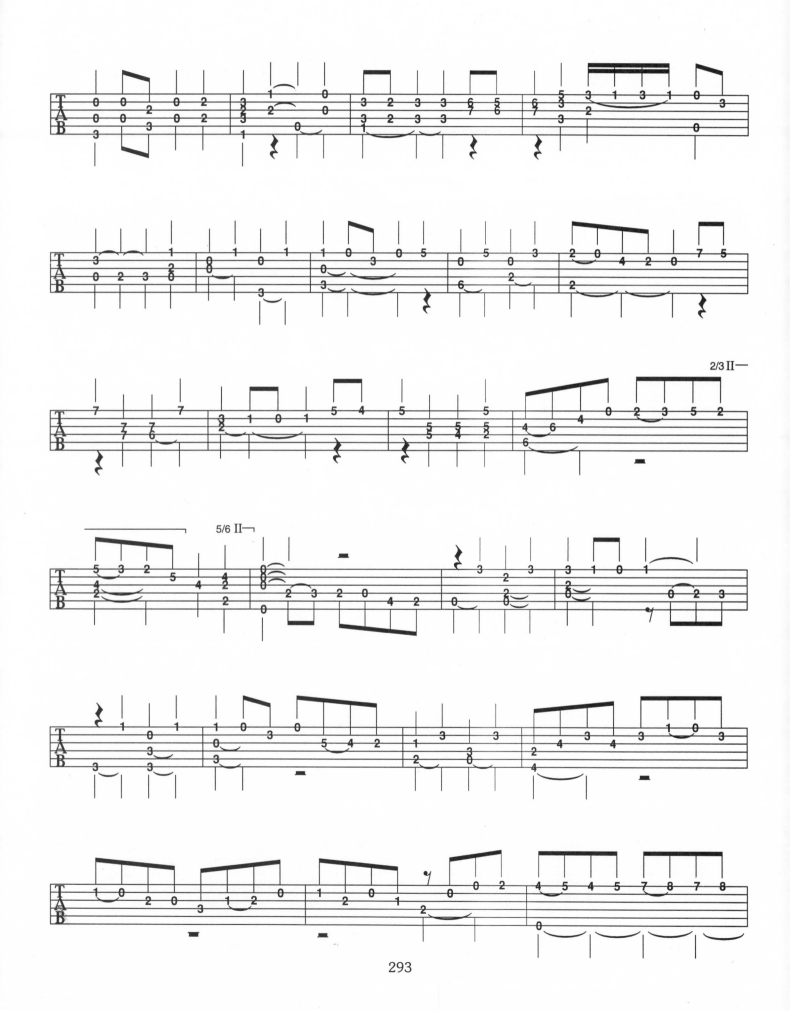

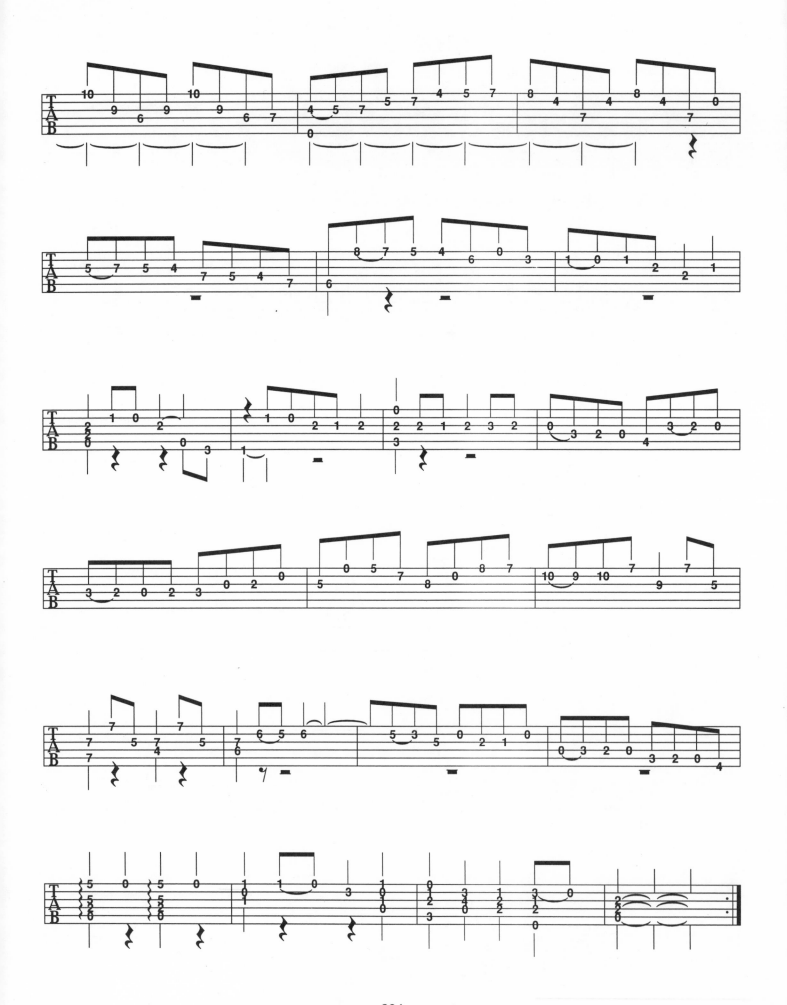